How Many Kinds of Animals Are There?

Are People Really Nine Feet Tall in Africa?

How Do Submarines Work?

ANSWERS
AND MORE ANSWERS

By Mary Elting
Illustrations by Tran Mawicke

GROSSET & DUNLAP
Publishers • NEW YORK

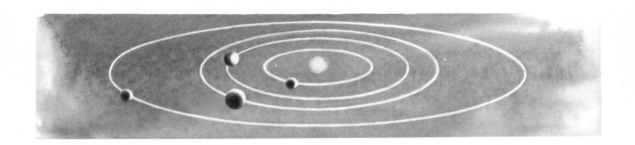

FOREWORD

Not long ago I wrote THE ANSWER BOOK, and soon after it appeared I began to get letters from readers. One of them said: "I asked your book a question, but it didn't tell me. Why do telephone wires hum?" Another said: "I liked your book because there were some answers my parents didn't know. Do you have any more answers?"

I did, indeed, have answers to more of the questions that boys and girls ask and keep on asking. Some of these questions were relayed to me by teachers. I want particularly to thank the following who have shared with me their knowledge of the things young people want to find out: Mr. Harold Mogin of Bridgewater-Raritan, New Jersey, High School; Mrs. Ilse Riesenfeld and Mr. Arthur A. Mitchell of Roosevelt, New Jersey, Public School.

The answers you will find here all came from people and from books. For help in tracking them down, I want to thank Mrs. Lore Phillips who has been both a resourceful and an energetic research assistant.

Finally, I owe a special debt of gratitude to Mr. Theodore Marton of Princeton University who took time to read the manuscript while he was completing experimental work on some of the problems of life in space. I am grateful to him for the zest with which he approached the task and for the many valuable suggestions he made.

Mary Elting

TO THE QUESTION-ASKERS

Boys and girls have always asked questions like "What makes the wind blow?"; "How does a bird fly?"; "What makes a cat purr?" Such questions are a normal part of growing up and becoming familiar with the world around you. Today, however, new knowledge is being discovered at such a rapid pace that there are even more questions to ask than in the past. Did you know that many of the everyday things you use today were unknown at the time your parents and grandparents were your age? Some of the new questions whose answers you will find in this book are: "What is a flying saucer?"; "What makes a submarine go up and down?"; "Why does a jet plane leave a trail in the sky?"

It is, therefore, more important today than it has ever been before for you to keep asking questions and to search in every way for the answers. Those Miss Elting has given in this book will satisfy a great need and should start you on your search for many more answers. For the quest for knowledge is a never-ending search for the truth, and in several areas of learning, men have only begun to explore the surface.

On the last pages, the author offers some ways in which you can satisfy your curiosity. She advises you to ask questions, to watch carefully and to try out explanations. I would emphasize the great importance of books. They will help to stretch your knowledge even further, because for many of the questions that the author answers, there is often an entire book devoted to the same subject.

For example, to answer more fully the question "What makes the wind blow?" there are *The How and Why Wonder Book of Weather* by George Bonsall; *My Easy-to-Read True Book of Air Around Us* by Margaret Friskey; and *Everyday Weather and How It Works* by Herman Schneider and J. Bendick. To answer one of the new questions like "Why does a jet plane leave a trail in the sky?" there are *Junior Science Book of Flying* by Rocco V. Feravolo; and *Rockets, Missiles, and Moons* by Charles Coombs. These and many others like them can be found in a school library or public library.

Mary Elting's *Answers and More Answers* and her earlier work *The Answer Book* will inform you about the wonders of the world in which we live. And if they start you on a quest for knowledge about new things, then they will have served another admirable purpose. Above all, keep your curiosity alive!

Mary Virginia Gaver, Professor, Graduate School of Library Service, Rutgers, The State University, New Brunswick, New Jersey

CONTENTS

ARE FLYING SAUCERS REAL?

MANY STRANGE things can be seen in the sky. When the weather is just right, circles of light that look like extra suns may be visible. Some people have called these lights flying saucers, but they are not saucers and they do not fly. Instead, they are reflections of the sun itself, made when the smooth faces of ice crystals act as mirrors high in the air.

Weather scientists often use plastic balloons to lift special instruments far above the earth. Many people think they are seeing a mysterious flying saucer when sunlight flashes from one of these shiny balloons.

If there is a layer of cool air near the ground and a layer of quiet, warm air above, a strange thing sometimes happens. The warm layer acts like a mirror, and reflections of moving automobile lights, hidden in the distance, look like objects flying through the sky.

Sometimes at night, balls of light appear over marshy places. Decaying material in the marsh produces a gas which can catch fire and burn with a weird light. In stormy weather, spots of blue light called St. Elmo's fire may appear around an airplane's propellers. These are just large sparks of electricity — the kind you make when you touch a metal doorknob after scuffing your feet along a thick rug.

Once in a while experts discover something that doesn't yet have a complete explanation. But so far, they have found no evidence of any flying objects from another world.

EVEN ON THE CLEAREST night, wisps of floating cloud and bits of dust pass between us and the stars. For a moment the starlight is dim, then bright again. These quick changes are twinkles. Light also bends and shimmers when it travels through different layers of cold and warm air. And inside our eyes, pinpoints of starlight may flicker on and off when they are not quite bright enough for us to see them steadily.

ARE THERE PEOPLE ON OTHER WORLDS?

MANY SCIENTISTS believe the chances are very good that creatures with brains live in other parts of the universe. For one thing, the materials of which we are made seem to exist in other parts of space. For another, many stars in the universe resemble our sun, and they were formed in the same way. There are millions of these other suns, and so there must be millions of planets. At least one of these many planets must be very much like the earth. If that is so, then living creatures *could* grow and develop in another world, just as they have in ours.

Many experts believe that tiny living things called microbes can travel safely in cold outer space. Perhaps these wanderers may carry life from one part of the universe to another. It is also possible that creatures very unlike ourselves can live and grow and have ideas, although they do not breathe our kind of air or eat our kind of food.

HOW COULD WE LEARN ABOUT PEOPLE ON OTHER PLANETS?

SUPPOSE someone on another planet invents radio and builds a very powerful broadcasting station. Suppose he wants to let us know that he exists. He could do this, even though he could not speak any of earth's languages. All he needs to do is send out radio signals that can be counted in some special order.

For example, he might send out *beep, beep-beep, beep-beep-beep*. This would show that he can count — 1, 2, 3. He could send 2 beeps, than 4, then 6, then 8, and so on. This would show that he can count by twos. Probably he would send much more complicated number-signals which only a scientist could recognize. Anyone who is able to invent radio must know a great deal about numbers and mathematics.

Some experts feel so sure that they will sooner or later get number-messages, they have set up a project for listening on the giant radio receivers that follow rockets and satellites in space.

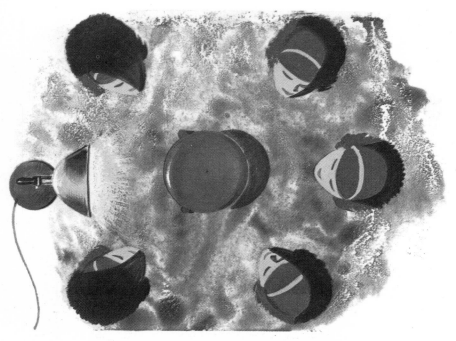

Pretend you are sitting on the stool in the center of the picture. As the girl moves in a circle, you turn on the stool, so you can watch her face.

WHY DOESN'T THE MOON ALWAYS LOOK ROUND?

SOMETIMES the moon shines round and full in the sky. Two weeks later, all you see is a golden sliver. In another two weeks it is full again, and in between times, the shape has changed from night to night. With a lamp, a stool and a friend to help, you can see why this happens. There are two things to know before you begin: First, the moon travels around the earth. Second, the moon does not glow with its own light. Moonshine is reflected sunshine.

Now, call the lamp the sun. You will be the earth, and your friend, the moon. Put the lamp behind you and sit on the stool facing your friend who stands looking over your head at the lamp. Her full face shines in the lamplight, like the full moon.

Tell your friend to move to her right in a circle around you, facing you all the time. You turn on the stool so that you are always facing her. After she has moved through one quarter of a circle, only her right cheek gets light from the lamp. The left cheek is now in shadow. See how the shadow gradually creeps across her nose, over onto the right cheek as she circles farther.

When she is halfway around the circle, no light falls on her face at all. Tell her to keep on moving. You will see a sliver of light appear on her left cheek, just the way the sliver of new moon shows up in the sky.

She keeps on circling. You see more of the left half of her face light up.

Finally, she comes back to where she started. The moon is full again.

14

WHAT IS A MERCURY CAPSULE?

A CAPSULE is a closed container that just fits the material it is made to hold. Does this mean that a Mercury capsule contains mercury? No, indeed! It is a container made to hold a space man and all the things he needs for rocketing into space and back again.

The name comes from old Greek stories about Mercury, the winged messenger, who was supposed to fly at a great speed back and forth between men on earth and the gods high above.

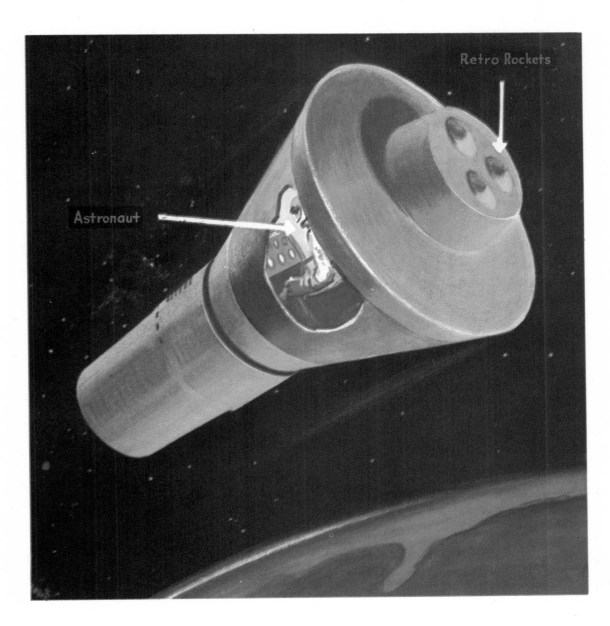

WHY DOES A MERCURY CAPSULE FLY BACKWARD?

A MERCURY capsule only *seems* to go in the wrong direction. We are used to seeing pointed noses on aircraft. The rocket that launches a space craft is pointed. But the capsule itself has a rounded nose, and it narrows down in the rear. This gives us the notion that it was made to fly backward. The astronaut in the capsule does face the rear. He can be made more comfortable that way. When he returns to earth, it is better for him to land on his back because his chair is specially made to take up some of the hard bump.

There is a good reason for the capsule's shape. When it gets back to the earth's atmosphere after a flight, it is traveling very fast. Air striking its surface at high speed makes it very hot. A pointed nose would allow air to flow around and strike every part of the capsule. But the wide, blunt nose stops some of the air, forces it back and makes it into a sort of bumper. This bumper of air takes up much heat. The heat is then scattered sideways, and much of it misses the back part of the capsule. Even with this protection, the back part gets red-hot. Inside the capsule are layers of fiber glass and other materials which keep out most of the heat, so that a space man can be fairly comfortable.

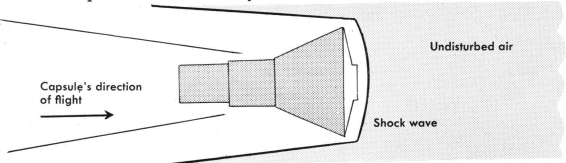

Capsule's direction of flight

Undisturbed air

Shock wave

WHAT IS A RETRO-ROCKET?

THE KIND OF ROCKET that carries a capsule out into space is called a *thrust* rocket. A *retro*-rocket is just the opposite. It acts as a brake on a capsule that is coming toward earth. *Retro* means backward or back. When a retro-rocket is fired, it pushes with great force against the capsule, and this slows the capsule's tremendous speed.

WHAT DOES COUNTDOWN MEAN?

WHEN RUNNERS get lined up for a foot race, the starter calls out, "On your mark! Get set! Go!"

When a rocket is going to be launched into space, the same kind of thing happens. A *Go!* signal will start the rocket on its way. But first the men who fire it must be sure that it is ready. They need many hours for this. They must check the complicated machinery that sets it off and guides it. The instruments that send radio messages back and forth have to be tested. All of this work has to be done at the right time. To make sure that it does get done, an announcer keeps telling the men how many hours and minutes are still left before firing time.

Then "T minus ten" comes over the radio loudspeakers. This means ten minutes are left. "T minus nine, T minus eight, T minus seven —" The minutes are counted down to one. From then on, seconds are counted. At "Time, zero!" the rocket kicks off.

Countdown is really a long and accurately timed "Ready! Get set! Go!"

WHAT IS A STAGED ROCKET?

WHEN A ROCKET starts toward space, it must have a big powerful engine to lift it from the earth. Such an engine uses a great deal of fuel, and fuel is heavy. The bigger the engine, the heavier its load of fuel must be.

But after the rocket has a good start, it does not need a big heavy engine. It would go faster with a lighter one. Of course, a rocket can't change engines in mid-air. But something else can be done. The heavy engine can actually be thrown away!

Rockets with throwaway engines are called *staged rockets*. They are built in several parts or stages. The bottom stage holds a big engine and much fuel, and it boosts the whole thing into the air. As soon as its fuel is gone, this stage is automatically blown off. At the same time, it lights a smaller engine which is carried with its own fuel in the next stage.

Space men have a name for the moment at which an engine's fuel is all gone. They call it *burnout*.

When the second stage reaches burnout, it drops off. A third engine starts. By now, the rocket is far above the earth, headed into space.

18

WHAT IS A SATELLOON?

"SATELLOON" is a new word made from two old ones — satellite and balloon. The balloon part of a satelloon may be as tall as a ten-story building. It has a skin of thin plastic covered with an even thinner layer of aluminum. It was made to travel around and around the earth, like an artificial moon. Scientists call an object a satellite when it goes through space in a regular path around the earth. And so this great shiny balloon got the name "satelloon."

The first satelloon was named *Echo*. A rocket carried it in a special container high above the earth. There the container opened, and Echo automatically expanded to full size. Then it began to circle the earth at about 16,000 miles an hour. Radio men used Echo for experiments with a radio telephone. From stations in New Jersey and California they broadcast phone conversations which bounced off Echo and were heard clearly all the way across the United States.

This is a huge receiver for radio telephone messages. First the messages are broadcast to a satelloon from a place on the earth. Then they bounce back to a different place where the receiver picks them up and sends them on to regular telephone wires. By radio and satelloon it is possible for a phone call to go all the way around the world.

19

WHY CAN'T WE SEE THE BACK OF THE MOON?

No ONE yet has actually seen the back of the moon. To understand why, get a friend to help you do an experiment. Pretend that you are the moon and he is the earth. Ask your friend to turn round and round, watching you at every turn. Now, with sideways steps, you circle around him. Keep your face toward him all the way, until you reach your starting point again. No matter which way he looks, your friend will never see the back of your head.

The moon travels around the earth in just the way you circled around your friend. The moon makes a complete circle once every twenty-nine and a half days.

Although no one has ever seen it, we do know what the back of the moon looks like. It has been photographed. Russian scientists sent a camera in a rocket around the invisible side. The camera took pictures, and these were broadcast to earth, by radio. The pictures show that the hidden side of the moon is a little smoother than the old familiar face.

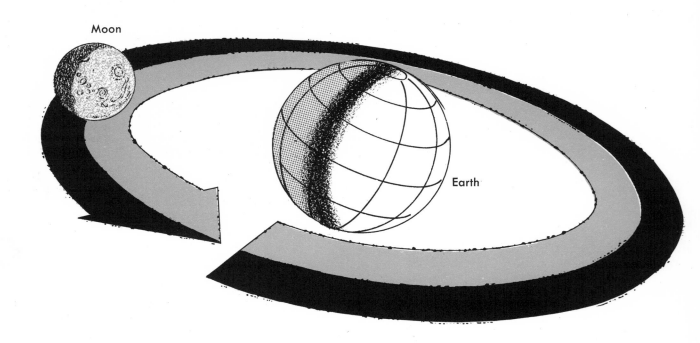

Moon

Earth

IT IS FUN to look at the dark smudges on the moon and imagine that they look like eyes and a nose and mouth. A long time ago, people who studied the moon thought that these smudges were seas. Scientists now know that there is no water on the moon, and the dark spots are really large flat plains. The biggest one is about 600 miles across.

WHY IS SUNSHINE HOT?

WHAT WE CALL sunshine has another name, too. Scientists call it radiation. There are different kinds of radiation. Light is one. Heat is another. Light and heat come from the sun at the same time. We see the light and feel the heat, and so we say that sunshine is hot. Another kind of radiation from the sun is invisible ultra violet light. It gives us a sun tan.

WHAT IS A SUNSPOT?

THERE ARE dark spots on the sun, like islands in a glowing, stormy sea. These spots could not be solid islands, of course. The sun is much too hot for that. It is so hot that everything in it and on it has been turned to gas. As the hot gases churn around, big patches of quieter, cooler gas form. These are the sunspots.

We still have much to learn about sunspots. Scientists know that gigantic electrical storms go on in the sun. Somehow these storms produce the dark spots which may last for a month or more before they vanish or move across the sun's face out of sight.

Sunspots seem to appear in great numbers about once every eleven years, but no one knows exactly why. We do know that powerful radio signals come from the sun during the electrical storms. These signals interfere with radio and television broadcasting on earth.

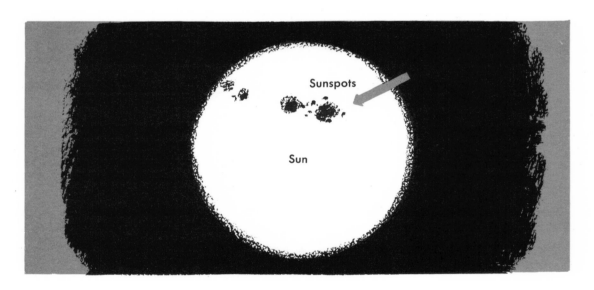

WILL THE SUN EVER GET COLD?

SEVERAL billion years from now, the sun may be just a cold, heavy lump. If it does end that way, the change will take a very, very long time. It may even get hotter before it grows colder. But you need not worry about feeling any difference in the sun's heat. The change will come so slowly that your great-grandchildren will not even notice it.

WHAT IS THE AURORA BOREALIS?

ANOTHER NAME for the Aurora Borealis is Northern Lights. People in northern countries often see this mysterious colored glow in the sky after dark. It sometimes appears as far south as Virginia. The glow may be blue or green or yellow-orange or red. Or it may be a combination of colors. Often it seems to rise and fall, like the swirling color in a neon light bulb. In fact, an aurora is a sort of giant neon sign!

A real neon light bulb contains a special kind of gas that glows when you turn on the electricity. There are gases floating above the earth, too, and electricity makes them give off light. Of course, nobody pushes a button to turn the Aurora on. The gases glow when they are hit by electric particles that come all the way from the sun.

Some of these particles shoot out from the sun every day. But sometimes the sun has great electrical storms. The storms fling out vast quantities of the particles, which gather in a ring high above the earth. When the ring gets too crowded, it spills over. Showers of particles fall toward the North Pole, and the Northern Lights go on. Particles that fall toward the South Pole cause another aurora above the southern part of the earth. It is called Aurora Australis.

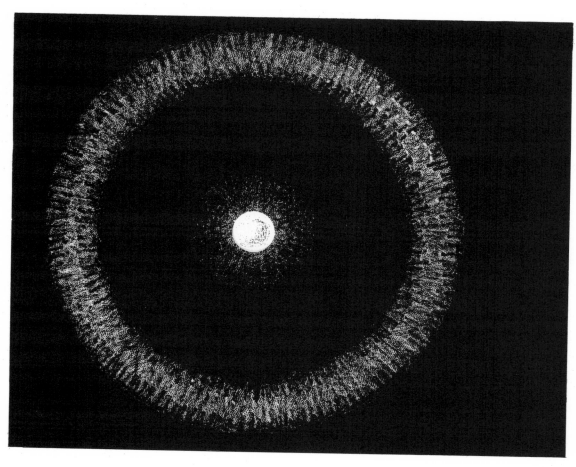

WHY DO WE SOMETIMES SEE A RING AROUND THE MOON?

A BIG RING of light sometimes appears around the moon. When this happens, you can be sure there is a thin cloud made of tiny ice crystals floating high in the air. Some of the light rays from the moon pass through or between the ice crystals. When these reach your eyes, you see the moon. But when other rays strike the crystals, a curious thing happens. Instead of going straight on, the rays are bent. When they reach your eyes, they seem to come from a circle that is much bigger than the moon.

Sometimes the ring is small. This means that moonlight has been bent by tiny water droplets high in the air.

Scientists call a big ring a *halo*. A small one is a *corona*.

Big rings and little rings appear around the sun, too — and for exactly the same reasons.

24

WHAT IS A COMET?

A COMET looks like nothing else you have ever seen in the night sky. It is a small bright speck at the center of a glowing, fiery ball, and it usually has a long, shining tail. What is it made of? A comet is a sort of huge, dirty snowball!

Scientists think that particles of gas, specks of dust and droplets of water all came together, long ago, far out in space. Somehow, these substances formed themselves into great frozen balls.

Comets travel through space, and some of them, we know, have regular paths around the sun, so that we see them again and again. What we see is really sunlight reflected from a cloud of vapor that streams out, all around the comet's cold inner ball. Some astronomers believe that comets may evaporate and disappear, but outer space is very cold, and so the process would probably take a long time.

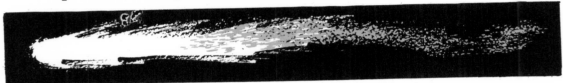

HOW MANY STARS ARE THERE IN THE SKY?

THE SKY at night shows us a great many stars. Yet it doesn't seem over-crowded, because we see only those stars which are largest or nearest. If we look through a big telescope, some of the dark empty spaces turn out to be filled with dots of light. Some of these dots are single stars that the eyes alone cannot see. Others are really whole groups of stars that look like a single star until we see them through an even larger telescope.

No one could hope to count the stars one by one. But there are telescopes combined with cameras that take pictures of the sky, and these photographs help sky watchers to do their complicated counting. Right now, they believe that there are about 100 billion stars in the group that the earth and sun belong to. This group is called a galaxy, and there are many other galaxies besides our own. Some are smaller, and some are much larger. The big telescopes and star-counting machines have shown that there must be at least a billion galaxies altogether!

IS A METEOR THE SAME AS A COMET?

METEORS are chunks of solid rock or metal that speed through space. Comets, too, move through space, but they are made of dust, ice and frozen gases.

Almost any clear night you can see at least one meteor flashing by. You probably call it by its other name — shooting star. Comets appear above the earth much less often, and as a rule, you need a telescope to see them.

A meteor leaves a fiery streak behind it when it comes close to the earth. It zips through the air so fast that it gets very hot. The tail of a comet is different. It shines in reflected sunlight.

Most meteors burn or explode while they are still in the air. A few fall to earth, and then they are called meteorites. One giant meteorite dropped onto the Arizona desert long ago and made a hole nearly a mile wide.

One night in the year 1908 something exploded in the air over Siberia. It knocked a whole forest down, lighted up the sky above half the earth, and disappeared without a trace. Russian scientists believe that a comet came too close to earth that night. It heated so quickly in the air that it exploded and vanished. The great blast of steam and gases blew the trees down flat for miles around.

The Great Meteor Crater in Arizona is nearly one mile wide.

WHAT IS A RADIO TELESCOPE?

AN ORDINARY TELESCOPE allows scientists to see light that comes from far out in space. A radio telescope detects things that cannot be seen. The fact is that stars give out radio waves as well as light, and there are clouds in space that send out radio waves but no light at all.

Some of these waves from space are strong enough to be heard with a regular radio receiver. Other waves are weak and have to be picked up by the huge dish-shaped radio telescopes. The dish collects many weak, scattered signals and focuses them together. A scientist does not actually look or listen through a radio telescope. But he does get information, and different radio telescope receivers give it to him in different ways. Some change the signals into wavy light on a screen. Others produce wavy lines on paper. Still others have mechanical brains that change the waves into numbers that are printed on paper. These waves and figures are a kind of code that experts can read.

Radio telescopes have another use, too. They pick up signals from man-made satellites in space. A small satellite with just a little battery can send back weak signals which the telescope can magnify. On page 13 you will find a picture of a huge radio telescope. The picture on this page shows another kind of receiver that picks up messages from satellites.

WHAT HAPPENS when a man weighs himself? Would you say that his body pushes down on the scales? That is one way of thinking about it. But you can also think about it in another way. The earth's gravity is pulling on the man, and the scales show how great that pull is.

Scientists do not yet know exactly what gravity is, but they have learned some of its rules. They know that a large ball of rock has a greater pull than a little ball made from the same kind of rock. The earth and the moon seem to be made of very similar material, but the moon is much smaller. Therefore, its pull is much less.

Suppose a man weighs 180 pounds on earth. On the moon, the pointer on the scales would go up to only 28 pounds!

Lunar Unicycle reproduced by courtesy of American Bosch-Arma Corp. and Frank Tinsley.

Since the pull of gravity is less on the moon than on earth, a man would fall more slowly if he jumped off a rock. A heavy exploring machine like the one in the picture could bounce along easily and lightly.

SUPPOSE a scientist wants to find out how much dust a space craft runs into between the earth and the moon. Before the craft leaves earth, he attaches a radio microphone inside its skin. Each time a particle of space dust hits the skin, the microphone senses it, and the radio in the craft broadcasts a signal back to earth. That's not all. The strength of the signal tells how large the bit of dust is.

A scientist may also want to know what happens to an animal's temperature when it travels in space. In order to find out, he can attach a special measuring instrument to the animal's body. This picks up heat just as a microphone picks up sound. The radio in the space craft then broadcasts signals that change as the animal's temperature goes up or down.

Power for broadcasting comes from batteries that are run by sunlight. On earth a special kind of receiver picks up the radio signals.

The signals often bring several different sorts of information at once. A mechanical brain separates the information and prints it on paper for the scientist to study!

This measuring of things at a distance by radio is called *telemetering*.

Once a scientist in Antarctica used a telemeter to study something altogether surprising — the temperature of penguin eggs. He stole one of two eggs from a nest, opened it, put in a tiny radio broadcasting device, and glued the egg together again. Then he put the telemeter egg back in the nest. The mother and father penguins took turns sitting on it, along with the other egg, which hatched after a while. Meantime, the scientist placed a radio antenna above the nest to pick up signals from the telemeter egg. He connected the antenna to a telemeter receiver indoors and studied the signals till the good egg hatched. He discovered that baby penguins can grow inside eggs, even though they are not kept as warm as the parents' own bodies.

WHY DOES A DOG WAG ITS TAIL?

Suppose one dog walks up to another, slowly waving his tail from side to side. Does this mean he is in a good mood and wants to make friends? An expert on dog behavior has found a surprising answer. This kind of tail wagging is a sign that the dog has a habit of bossing other dogs. If the newcomer is used to giving in, the two will probably get along together. But if the newcomer also gives a boss-dog wag, a fight may easily start. A tail that wags while it is tucked down close to the legs often belongs to a dog that is used to obeying. It is a sign that he won't demand his own way.

Some tail wagging, of course, goes along with pleasure. But it is not something a dog does because he wants to show how glad he is to see you. The motion of his tail starts automatically when his eyes tell his brain that you are there. Scientists have not done much experimenting to find out what gives animals pleasure or why they show it in different ways.

WHY DO CATS PURR?

A cat purrs when it is relaxed and comfortable. Purring is something that cat ancestors began to do long, long ago. No one knows why purring started or why it goes on.

WHY DO TAME ANIMALS FIGHT?

Two PUPPIES are playing together. The next minute they may be fighting. One of them may have nipped the other too hard. All animals, tame or wild, try to protect themselves. They are likely to go into action when they feel pain. At the same time, pain actually helps their muscles to get extra power and speed. Pain is like a trigger that fires a gun filled with strength-making chemicals. The "guns" are little pouches called glands.

In many animals, pain is not the only trigger. A certain sound or smell may shoot the chemical gun. Even the sight of another animal may trigger the glands and make them work just as they work when there is pain. This often means "Fight!" Scientists do not yet know all of the things that act as triggers, but they have not found proof that animals have any wild, mysterious need to fight.

A dog doesn't stop and figure out the best way to get rid of something that threatens to hurt him. His glands, not his brains, send him into action. One animal does have a brain that can solve problems by thinking instead of fighting. That animal is man. Of course, people get angry and fight. But when they do, they, too, are being ruled by their glands, instead of their brains!

Elephants have a peculiar gland between the eye and the ear. Sometimes it swells up — no one knows why — and a kind of oil oozes from it. When this happens an elephant trainer is very cautious. At any minute the large, gentle animal may get into a terrible rage and attack its best friends.

YOUR DOG is asleep. Suddenly his legs twitch and he makes little excited sounds. It seems that he must be dreaming of chasing a rabbit or perhaps running after another dog. But we do not really know, because he cannot tell us after he wakes up. Even though your dog may seem to be almost human sometimes, his brain is different from yours. What goes on when he whines and moves in his sleep may not be the same thing that goes on in your brain when you dream.

A cat's sweat glands are in the soft pads on the bottom of its feet.

WHY DO DOGS PANT?

PANTING keeps a dog's body from getting too hot. You don't have to pant on a warm day, because many small sweat glands in your skin help to keep your body at the right temperature. The sweat glands open up and let tiny drops of moisture escape into the air. When a drop of sweat flies away, it leaves your skin a little cooler. A fan blowing a current of air over you carries away sweat quickly, and so it makes you very cool.

A dog has very few sweat glands, but if he breathes hard, his breath is a current of air that blows away moisture from his lungs and mouth. Panting works for a dog just as an electric fan works for you!

A dog sometimes pants in a hot room on a winter day. His fur coat is keeping him too warm. *You* can take your coat off, but your dog has to turn on his panting-fan instead.

ARE RACE HORSES DIFFERENT FROM OTHER HORSES?

RACE HORSES are different from other horses in one important way. They can run faster. People raise them for speed and speed alone, and they aren't much good for anything else. Here is the story of the most famous kind of race horse:

About three hundred years ago, an English king, Charles II, got three fine stallions from different countries. One of them was Turkish, one was Arabian and one North African. He mated these stallions with his best English mares. After a hundred years, their descendants were the fastest racers in England. They became known as Thoroughbreds.

Look at the picture and you will see that a Thoroughbred has its own special appearance. Other horses are stronger. Other horses are tougher. Others are better for all-around riding. But no other kind of horse can carry a rider as fast in a long race as a Thoroughbred can.

DO BULLS ATTACK WHEN THEY SEE RED?

THE CUSTOM of waving a red cape in front of a bull during a bullfight is so old that no one would think of changing it. But anything that moves would attract the bull's attention just as well. And either a white or a black cape would work best of all. Bulls cannot tell one color from another. Neither can cows. So everything appears black or white or gray — exactly as it does when you see a color television show on an ordinary black-and-white screen.

Dogs, cats, horses and many other animals have no color vision. Snakes do see in color. So do fish and some insects and birds that are active in daytime.

HOW DID ANIMALS GET TO BE TAME?

IN THE DAYS before anyone in the world knew how to farm, people got their food by hunting and collecting wild seeds and roots. Scientists believe that men often brought the puppies of wild dogs and wolves back from hunting trips. As these puppies grew up in the camps, some probably ran off and returned to the woods. Some may have been too fierce to have around. Men probably killed these. But some were gentle. They grew used to the ways of men. They stayed in the camps and had puppies of their own. In this way, special kinds of dogs developed — dogs that were tame and depended on human beings.

No one knows exactly when or where men captured and brought up the first wild puppies. It probably happened many times in many different places. But we do think that dogs were the very first animals to be tamed. *Domesticated* is another word that means tamed.

The next animal to be domesticated was the goat, and we know a little more about where and when this happened. Long ago a certain kind of wild goat roamed the hills in countries we now call Israel and Syria and Iraq and Iran. The people in these hills gathered wild wheat and wild barley for food. Then they discovered they could plant the grain and raise crops. Goats liked wheat and barley, too, so some of them began to live near villages where people grew the grain. The villagers found it was handy to have the goats near by. Goats were good to eat. So people began to take care of them and to drive away the animals that attacked them. In this way, goats were domesticated about 7,000 years ago.

Soon afterward, men in the same hilly country started herding and protecting wild sheep. Next they fed and protected wild pigs and cattle. About five thousand years ago, the people in that same part of the world first captured and trained wild asses and wild horses.

AMERICAN SADDLE HORSE. This breed developed in Kentucky in pioneer days, when a good riding horse was very important, because there were no roads.

TENNESSEE WALKING HORSE. Long ago, men in the southern part of the United States bred horses that gave them an easy ride as they went around slowly inspecting their large plantations.

STANDARDBRED. A race horse that pulls a small two-wheeled cart called a sulky. Some Standardbred horses race at a very fast trot. That means the horse always has a forefoot and a hind foot on opposite sides off the ground at the same time. Other Standardbred horses are pacers. When a horse paces, it puts forward both feet on the same side at the same time.

QUARTER HORSE. American horse-racing tracks in the old days were not big. Gradually, men bred horses that were particularly fast in races only a quarter-mile long. These became known as quarter horses. Since they can make quick starts, they are useful to cowboys for herding and roping cattle.

IS A PONY THE SAME AS A HORSE?

A LITTLE Shetland pony looks very different from a saddle horse or a huge Percheron, but all three are true horses. Each one has its own appearance and size, because men needed or wanted it that way.

When people want big horses, they choose their largest ones to be the mother and father of new baby horses, which are called foals. After the foals grow up, the largest of them are chosen to have young of their own, and so on, time after time, until the horse raisers have developed just the kind of big, strong horse they want.

Long ago, men developed the Percherons to carry knights into battle. A knight wore a great heavy suit of metal armor, and so his horse had to be large and powerful. Later, the Percherons became useful farm animals.

ARABIAN. People who lived in the desert of Arabia bred horses that had great endurance and intelligence. An Arabian horse has one less bone in its back than most other breeds.

PERCHERON. This huge horse was bred for strength, and it is still used instead of a tractor on some farms in this country. A Percheron often weighs twice as much as most saddle horses.

MORGAN. Old-time farmers in Vermont could not afford to keep several different kinds of horses. They developed the Morgan, which was good for riding, pulling light buggies, and doing farm work.

BELGIAN. The biggest of all horses are the Belgians which pull heavy wagons and do farm work.

THOROUGHBRED. The famous saddle horse that was developed for speed.

SHETLAND PONY. These are the smallest of all horses. Some are no bigger than a large dog.

People on the Shetland Islands near Scotland had a different problem. Their land did not grow enough food for big horses with large appetites. So they developed their famous little ponies. In other places, Shetlands were used to pull cars in mine tunnels, where there wasn't much room. A pony is any fullgrown horse that measures less than four feet six inches tall at its shoulder.

People have created many different kinds of horses. Some are good long-distance runners. Some can do best in short races. Some are raised mainly for the way they look. When mother and father horses (called mares and stallions) keep on having foals that are just like themselves, we say these horses have become a separate *breed*. When a mare and stallion of the same breed have a foal, we say the foal is *purebred*.

CAN A DOG FOLLOW A TRAIL WITH ITS NOSE?

PEOPLE have a better sense of smell than a great many other animals, but dogs have better noses than people. They can sense odors that we don't even know exist. Hunters all over the world have found that dogs can pick up the very faint smell left by other animals, and they can follow the trail sometimes for miles. In the Far North, dogs lead Eskimos to the breathing holes that seals make in the ice. Whether the dog smells the seal or only the ocean water, nobody knows for sure. We do know his sense of smell is better than his master's because the inside of his nose is longer, and it has many more of the little sensitive spots where an odor can be picked up.

Salmon can also follow an odor trail. They can smell the difference between the water in one stream and the water in another stream nearby. This ability may explain a great mystery about salmon on the northwest coast of America. These big fish hatch out of eggs in fresh water, far from the ocean. Then young salmon swim down river to the sea where they live for several years. At the end of this time, they swim back hundreds of miles to the very spot where they were born, and there they lay their own eggs. Apparently the salmon's ability to smell out different kinds of water helps it to find its way home.

WHY DOES A COW CHEW ITS CUD?

MAYBE SOMEONE has told you that a cow has four stomachs. Actually a cow has only one stomach, but that one is divided into four pouches.

When a cow takes a bite of grass, she does not stop to chew it. She swallows it right away, and it goes down into the first of her four stomach pouches. Later, while she is resting, she brings the wadded grass back up to her mouth. This wad is called a cud. The cow chews the cud thoroughly, and mixes it in her mouth with a liquid called saliva. Chemicals in the saliva start to change the grass so that her body can use it.

When the cow finishes chewing a cud, she swallows it. This time it goes into the second stomach pouch. A special valve closes off the first one. From the second pouch, the grass goes into the third and then into the fourth. In each of these pouches, it mixes with more chemicals. Finally the nourishment from the grass is all ready for the cow to use. Altogether a cow spends about nine hours of every twenty-four in cud-chewing.

A four-in-one stomach was a help to a cow's wild ancestors who had to watch out for enemies. Wild cattle could snatch up grass in a hurry, then go out of sight and chew their cuds in peace.

Usually just one yolk at a time goes down the tube. But sometimes two yolks start out very close together. Then one shell surrounds both, and the hen lays a double-yolk egg.

HOW DOES A HEN LAY AN EGG?

INSIDE A HEN is a sack called an ovary. There, tiny little egg yolks form and start to grow. When a yolk has reached its full size, it enters a long tube. Soon the white part of the egg oozes from the sides of the tube and surrounds the yolk. When the egg comes close to the end of the tube, it gets a coating of calcium. This substance hardens and makes the shell. Now, muscles push the finished egg out of the hen's body.

Inside the yolk of an egg is the germ of a new chicken. The yolk and the white are food the chick will grow on before it hatches.

New eggs to make new chickens keep coming from hens all through the year. Men have developed this special kind of bird that can keep on laying eggs day after day. Wild birds lay their eggs only during the nesting season.

HOW DO MOTHER ANIMALS KNOW THEIR OWN BABIES?

HUNDREDS of baby lambs live with their mothers in large flocks. Each lamb seems to us exactly like all the others. But a mother sheep knows the difference. No matter how many lambs there are in the flock, she can always pick out her own baby, because it has its own particular odor. The minute a lamb is born, the mother sniffs it. From then on, she remembers exactly how it smells.

Deer and buffalo, cats, dogs and many, many other animal mothers know their babies by smell.

A mother penguin knows her own chick. Dozens of chicks stay together in groups while the grown-up birds go fishing in the ocean for food. When a mother gets back, she waddles through the whole hungry crowd of babies and refuses to feed any but her own. People who study penguins aren't quite sure, but they think the mother and father both recognize their baby's voice and also its own particular shape and size and look.

A baby penguin seems to recognize its parents' voices. When its mother or father calls, it comes running. When a baby chick or duck hatches, it usually sees first of all the big dark shape of its mother. From then on, it recognizes that shape and follows it. But if ducklings happen to see a dog's shape first, they will follow the dog around just as if it were their mother. They will even follow a large stout scientist who is experimenting with ducks — if they see him first.

41

WHAT MAKES ELECTRICITY IN ELECTRIC EELS?

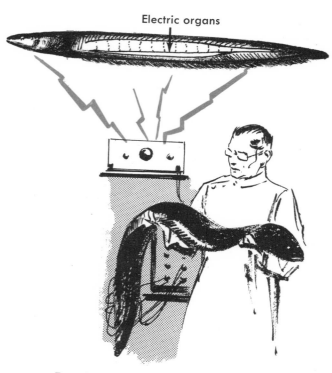

Electric organs

Experimenters still need to find out more about electricity in eels and in other animals, too. They know that all living things, including people, have electricity in their bodies. They know that chemicals in the body can change into other chemicals, and this has something to do with making electricity travel through the nerves. Many scientists are at work studying the electric currents in human beings. Perhaps when they learn more about people, they will know more about electric eels, too.

MORE THAN HALF of an electric eel's body is arranged somewhat like an automobile battery. It has rows and rows of small, thin plates with a liquid around them. In a battery, the plates are made of metal. In an eel, they are made of living stuff, something like muscle.

To get a strong electric current from several batteries, you can connect them with copper wire. An eel's electric parts are connected in the same way! Living cords, called nerves, take the place of wires.

The eel can make an electric current flow in a circular path from its head, through the water, to its tail, and back through its body to the head. This current can be strong enough to throw a man across the room. Scientists have managed to light electric bulbs with it. They are careful to wear rubber gloves which keep them from getting shocked.

Electric eel is not really the right name for this creature. Although it does resemble members of the eel family, in some ways it is more like a fish. But unlike a fish, it has no gills for breathing. Instead, it comes to the surface of the water and takes in gulps of air.

Gecko Lizard

CAN LIZARDS GROW NEW TAILS?

SOME LIZARDS have a very good way of escaping their enemies. If you catch one of them by the tail, the tail is all you catch! It breaks off and the lizard gets away. After a while a brand-new tail will grow.

A lizard is not the only animal that can grow a new part of its body. A starfish can grow a new arm when one is chopped off. And if a starfish is cut into two or three pieces, each with a part of the center attached, each piece can grow into a complete new starfish! There is one kind of worm that is even more surprising. It can learn to follow a certain regular path in order to get food. Then when it is cut in half, two new worms will grow, and *both* will remember the path that leads to food.

These animals are all much simpler than people or the other warm-blooded animals. A dog cannot grow a new tail, and we cannot replace a lost finger, although our bodies heal cuts and mend broken bones.

43

WHY DO WILD ANIMALS BECOME EXTINCT?

EVERYTHING in nature is always changing. Some kinds of animals are always dying out — becoming extinct. And, of course, new kinds are always appearing.

There are many different things that can cause all the animals of one particular kind to disappear. Scientists know some of the causes, but they don't yet know others. For instance, they can tell part of the story about the whooping cranes. These are very tall birds that spend the summers in northern Canada and winters in southern Texas. Only about two dozen of the big beautiful cranes are left. Soon there may be none.

Hunters with guns helped to make the whooping crane almost extinct, but there seems to be something else going on, too. Here is a mystery that scientists have not yet solved. In some years the flock has no new baby whooping cranes along when it flies south for the winter. Does this mean that no eggs have hatched, or that some disease or some wild enemy has killed the young birds after they hatched? Or does it mean that human hunters are killing the young birds before they can fly? Nobody knows.

Hunters nearly killed off the American buffalo. They shot almost all the thirty million of these big animals that once roamed the Great Plains.

Farmers, without meaning to do so, may help kill off certain kinds of animals or birds. The early pioneers used to see billions of big passenger

44

pigeons in the woods of Pennsylvania and New York State. Later countless numbers of these birds died of hunger. They could not get the food they needed, after men had cut down whole forests to get land for farms. Hunters also killed the birds by the million. The last passenger pigeon died in the Cincinnati Zoo in 1914.

Men were also responsible for killing off a bird called the dodo that lived only on the island of Mauritius, near Africa. This bird could not fly, and it built its nest on the ground. When newcomers brought in pigs, the pigs soon wiped out every single dodo on the island — and in the world.

Mammoths and mastodons used to live in North America. Ancient Indian hunters drove whole herds of them over cliffs or into swamps where it was easy to kill them. Some experts think that this was one of the reasons why the animals became extinct. Other experts think mammoths and mastodons would have died out anyway because the climate changed and the plants they ate no longer grew in their feeding grounds.

A change in climate may be the reason why dinosaurs and other strange prehistoric animals became extinct millions of years ago. Scientists are not sure about this. But as a general rule, they believe that animals die out when they don't change enough to keep up with changing conditions around them. Scientists also say that animals die out when they change so much that they can't fit into the world where they have to live.

WHY DO CATS' EYES SHINE AT NIGHT?

A CAT'S EYES in the daytime are like round windows with curtains pulled almost together in the middle. The cat sees through narrow slits that let light into the eyes. But at night the slits widen — the curtains pull back. Now the cat sees through much more of the round window, and it sees very well in a dim light — much better than we do. The reason is that the backs of the eyes are lined with little bits of shiny stuff, like thousands of mirrors. If there is even a dull gleam of light, each shiny mirror in the eyes catches the gleam and concentrates it. A scurrying mouse at night looks very dim to us, but it appears many times brighter to a cat.

When you see a cat's eyes glowing beside the road at night, the little inside mirrors are reflecting your flashlight or the headlights of a car. If you are in a completely dark place with a cat, its eyes do not shine at all, because there is no light to reflect. Cats cannot see in complete darkness, any more than we can. But their special kind of eyesight works so well that they can hunt at night.

HOW DO CHICKENS KNOW WHEN IT IS TIME TO GO TO BED?

CHICKENS and pigeons and many other birds go to sleep when it gets dark because there is nothing else they can do. Their eyes are not made for seeing in dim light. A chicken's eye is a daytime eye. It has none of the tiny special parts that make it possible for an owl or a cat to see to go hunting in dim light.

46

HOW FAST CAN FISH SWIM?

THE FASTEST FISH is the barracuda, so far as anyone knows. A four-foot-long barracuda can go twenty-seven miles an hour for short distances.

If you like to fish, you may think that trout are fast swimmers, but a nine-inch trout can only go about six miles an hour. A six-inch trout is even slower. It can go only four miles an hour. That's close to the speed of the fastest human swimmer.

Barracuda

DO BUGS HAVE BONES?

THE BONES inside your body contain a hard white stuff that is very much like a certain kind of rock. Your bones are called your skeleton, and your muscles are attached to it. An insect also has a hard skeleton, and it, too, is an anchor for muscles. But instead of being on the inside, it is on the outside — like a suit of armor that protects the soft inner parts. The armor is made of chemicals somewhat like the chemicals in fingernails. So, although bugs and other insects have skeletons, we can't say that they have bones.

SOME BIRDS don't have to to go south in winter, because they can find all the food they need, even when the ground is covered with snow. Chickadees, for instance, eat insect eggs that they find under the bark of trees. So do nuthatches and titmice. These birds can get the water they need by eating snow. They stay in sheltered spots at night or during storms.

Other birds can stay in the north because people set up feeding stations for them. Some of them have to be given water, too, because they don't eat snow.

WHY DOES A WOODPECKER PECK?

A DOWNY WOODPECKER drills holes in trees where wormlike wood-borer grubs live. His bill breaks into the grub's tunnel, and out goes his long tongue that is covered with sharp little hooks. The next moment the grub has been snagged, pulled out, and eaten.

A carpenter woodpecker likes nuts. He drills holes in an oak tree, stuffs an acorn in each one, then comes back later to chisel open the nuts for a feast.

A sapsucker is a woodpecker that drills for sap. The neat rows of holes you see in birch and other trees are the work of this thirsty drinker of juice.

All woodpeckers chop and pick and dig holes in trees or telephone poles where they build nests.

Most woodpeckers also do a great deal of plain, noisy drumming. Usually they drum on a dead branch or a hollow tree trunk. But sometimes they choose metal roofs or television aerials and they often go on for hours. Naturalists think a male woodpecker drums for the same reason that many other male birds sing. He is letting other woodpeckers know that this particular part of the world belongs to him and his family. No trespassing allowed!

Flicker

Pileated Woodpecker

Hairy Woodpecker

Red-Bellied Woodpecker

Red-Headed Woodpecker

TRAINERS teach wild animals in much the same way that you teach pets. You give a dog a reward when he does something right. You feed him or pat him. If he does something wrong, you show him that you disapprove. You may scold him or give him a swat. Gradually the dog gets into the habit of doing things that bring pleasant results, and he avoids the things that bring unpleasant ones.

A wild animal trainer gives a reward when an animal behaves in a tame way and punishment when it acts wild. Lions get meat for doing things right. Seals get fish. An elephant gets a lump of sugar.

Once a circus man trained a group of elephants to play ball. After they got used to taking orders from him, he started the ball-playing lessons. At first he held the bat and an elephant's trunk in his hands, both together. When a helper tossed a ball, the trainer swung at it. After each swing, he passed out rewards. Finally, the elephant discovered what the trainer wanted. From then on, he batted enthusiastically, all by himself. With the same sort of help, the rest of the elephant team were trained to throw the ball and run after it. The lessons took a long time, but in the end, the players could put on a good show.

Most animals have natural patterns in the way they behave. A good trainer watches for these patterns and uses them. For instance, a wild elephant does many things with its trunk, and with these same motions a tame elephant can perform tricks. Some animals have patterns that are easy for a trainer to use. Others are born with the kind of make-up that doesn't seem to tame easily — or at all.

WHY DOES AFRICA HAVE SO MANY WILD ANIMALS?

FOR THOUSANDS of years, African hunters used only spears and arrows and simple traps to get meat for their families. In all those years, vast numbers of buffalo, rhinoceros, antelope and other animals roamed the grassy plains or lived in forests where the trees were widely scattered. Elephants tramped the forests and bulldozed their way through rain-soaked jungles, and hippopotamuses swarmed in rivers and lakes.

People did not have such an easy time, and groups of human beings did not grow very large. The few hunters with their poor weapons could not destroy the huge herds. That is one reason why parts of Africa had great numbers of wild animals when the first European explorers arrived.

There are still many wild animals in certain places, but not nearly so many as there used to be. Man-made forest fires and grass fires have killed large numbers of them. White hunters with modern rifles have completely destroyed some kinds. African hunters have found they could get money they need by killing wild animals and selling the meat and the hides. This has also helped to cut down the size of the herds. In some places, though, governments are protecting the game. Only a certain number of animals can be killed each year. One protected place is as large as the state of Massachusetts. And so there are many wild animals left in Africa.

All of Africa's animals are badly needed, scientists say. Much of the land where the wild herds find plenty of food is no good for farming or ranching. In fact, the particular kind of soil there turns to barren desert when farm crops are planted on it. The experts say that Africans should protect their big wild animals, then harvest them each year according to a careful plan. This will give them more meat than if they try to raise tame animals where wild animals now live.

51

An oriole weaves its basket nest from grass and any stringy stuff it finds.

A hummingbird coats the outside of the nest with silk from a spider web or caterpillar cocoon. Then it adds flakes of gray lichen from rocks. The lichen clings to the silk, and you can hardly tell the nest from the tree branch.

HOW DO BIRDS LEARN TO BUILD NESTS?

BIRDS make many kinds of nests. An oriole weaves a basket. One kind of swallow digs a tunnel. A water bird called a horned grebe builds a nest that floats. The beautiful pink flamingo piles mud up high in a flat-topped mound, then it lays a single egg on top of that. There are even birds called weavers that build apartment houses. Two dozen or more of them work together on one big nest that has several separate rooms inside.

52

A *bank swallow* digs a tunnel more than a yard long in a steep bank of earth. At the end of the tunnel it makes a bed of feathers and grass.

A *hammerhead* builds a huge nest of mud and sticks and covers it with a roof so strong that you can stand on it.

A *chimney swift* really does live in a chimney. It makes a basket of sticks which it glues together with a liquid from its mouth. The same "glue" holds the nest to the steep wall of the chimney.

Human beings lived on the earth a long time before they learned how to build houses that are as complicated as some bird nests. If people are so slow, how do birds ever learn to make their wonderful homes?

A bird doesn't learn nest-building. When the time comes to build a nest, suddenly the bird knows how. The knowledge is already stored in its brain. We haven't yet discovered how this kind of knowledge gets stored, but one thing seems certain: no bird ever has to take a lesson in how to make a nest.

ARE TOADS THE SAME AS FROGS?

FROGS AND TOADS are close relatives, and it is often hard to tell them apart. If you see a chunky fellow covered with bumps that look like warts, it is likely to be a toad. Frogs are usually smoother and more slender. Most toads and frogs lay their eggs in water. The eggs hatch into tadpoles that swim about, looking like tiny fish until their legs develop. After they are grown up, toads usually live on land. Most frogs stay in or near water.

The warts on a toad's back won't give you warts if you touch them. But you should be careful about a white liquid that may ooze from the warts when you pick up a toad. The liquid can hurt your eyes or mouth, just as it hurts a toad's enemy. A raccoon may eat a toad after rolling it over and over to get rid of the disagreeable juice. Puppies soon learn to leave the creatures alone.

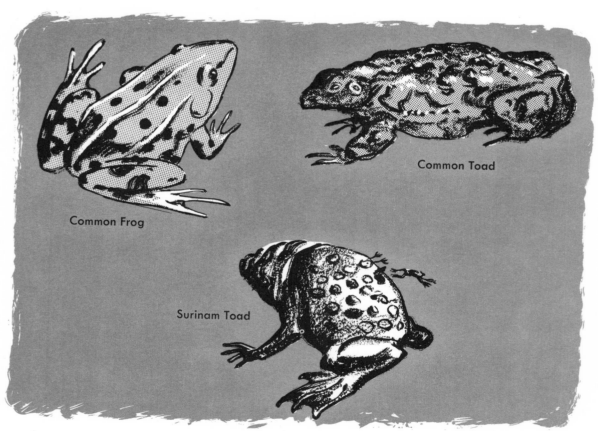

Common Frog

Common Toad

Surinam Toad

The Surinam toads in South America take care of their eggs instead of leaving them in the water. The male puts the eggs into little pouches on the female's back. When the tadpoles hatch, they stay in the pouches until they change into little toads. The babies then hop out and go their own way.

IS A TURTLE THE SAME AS A TORTOISE?

THERE WAS a time when scientists used separate names for the turtle and each of its two close relatives. The *turtle,* they said, was a large animal that lived in the sea and had flippers for swimming. The one that lived on land was a *tortoise.* The cousin that lived in fresh water was a *terrapin.* But people seem to like the name turtle best, and nowadays it is correct to use it for all three animals.

Green Turtle

Galapagos Tortoise

Diamondback Terrapin

HOW MANY ANIMALS ARE THERE IN THE WORLD?

IT IS IMPOSSIBLE to count all the land animals, all the fish in the ocean, all the birds in the air, not to mention the insects, the creepers, the crawlers and the animals too small even to be seen. No one can possibly know how many individual creatures there are. But scientists have counted the different species of animals they have found. Two animals belong to the same species when they can mate and have babies that can themselves have babies. Robins, hummingbirds and pelicans are all birds, but they belong to three different species.

About 8,700 species of birds have been listed and 4,500 species of mammals — that is, animals whose babies are fed on their mothers' milk. In summer you probably feel that there are more insects than anything else. Some scientists believe that at least 700,000 different species of insects have been discovered. Adding these to the fish and snakes and all other members of the animal kingdom, we get a total of about 900,000 different species in the world.

WHY ARE MOTHER AND FATHER BIRDS DIFFERENT COLORS?

SOME male and female birds look almost exactly alike, but others have feathers of different colors. The male is usually the brightly colored one. His fine feathers help to attract the female bird in the mating season. When it comes time to keep the eggs warm in the nest, the female does the sitting. Her dull color makes her and the nest and the eggs hard to see. She is safer from certain enemies than she would be if she had bright colored feathers. Male birds with brilliant coats seldom sit on nests. It would not be safe for them to do so.

Male Cardinal

Female

Male Bluebird

Female

Male Robin

Female Robin nesting

WHY DO BIRDS SING?

Birds give their calls in order to communicate with other birds. When the calls sound musical to our ears, we say they are songs.

A male bird may sing to attract a mate. Or he may sing to warn other males that they must stay out of a certain part of the woods or fields that he claims for himself. He may warn others away from a birdhouse in your back yard, too.

Some birds have calls they use to announce that they have discovered food. A crow uses a special sound to bring a flock of crows together.

Canaries in cages can't accomplish anything by singing, but they sing anyway. When a bird raiser finds canaries that do well in captivity, he keeps mating them until he gets really good singers. Sometimes he helps them along by letting young birds grow up near older ones that have lovely songs.

Many birds have warning cries. A European chaffinch uses one kind of call to warn its companions that an enemy bird is perched on a limb. But if the enemy is flying, the chaffinch gives a different warning call. One kind of bird called the guacharo lives in caves in South America. It makes clicking noises that help it to find its way in total darkness. Echoes from the clicks tell a guacharo when it must swerve in order to avoid a cave wall.

Canaries

Crow

Chaffinch

Guacharo

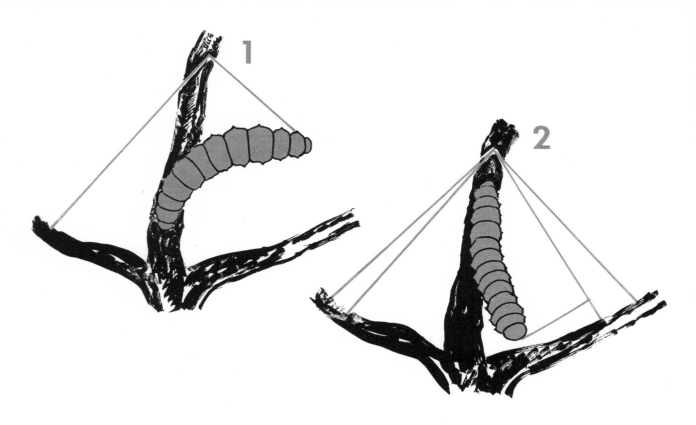

HOW DO CATERPILLARS SPIN COCOONS?

A COCOON is a sleeping bag where a caterpillar rests while it is changing into a moth. The caterpillar makes the cocoon around itself. When it finishes, it is completely wrapped up in its bag of soft silk.

The caterpillars that spin cocoons are also called silkworms. They make their silk from a sticky liquid that forms in sacks inside their mouths. This liquid hardens as soon as it comes out into the air. Using two front feet, a caterpillar can draw the silk from its mouth in a fine, long thread.

Different silkworms shape their cocoons differently. The pictures show a Cecropia caterpillar at work. First it grips a twig with its back feet, leaving the rest of its body free to move. Next it fastens a thread to the twig. Then it bends downward to one side in almost a half-circle, spinning out a length of thread which it fastens to the twig near its back feet. After several of these long, sweeping motions, it has a kind of framework to use. Now the caterpillar turns around on the twig and hangs upside down. Its head moves back and forth to put a floor in the cocoon. Again it turns, and clinging rightside up, it spins loops of thread to fill in the spaces between the framework threads.

58

Like any good sleeping bag, the cocoon has separate layers. First comes a thin, tough outside covering; next a fine, loose padding; then an inner envelope. Somehow a caterpillar can measure its silk as it spins. It stops work on the padding at just the right point, so that it has enough thread left to finish the inside cover! The Cecropia uses about 1,000 feet of thread altogether in the cocoon.

The Cecropia is a wild caterpillar that you can find in the woods. There are tame silkworms, too. People raise them specially to spin cocoons which are unraveled and made into silk cloth.

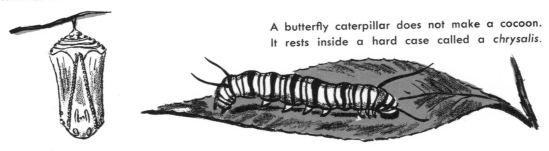

A butterfly caterpillar does not make a cocoon. It rests inside a hard case called a *chrysalis*.

IF YOU CUT AN EARTHWORM IN TWO, WILL THE PARTS GROW INTO TWO NEW WORMS?

No! BOTH PARTS will wiggle for a while, but at least one part will die.

If you look at an earthworm, you will see that it is made of many sections strung along one after another. If you cut off a few of the front sections, four or five of them will grow back. A worm can also grow back part of its tail sections if some of them get cut off. A worm can grow a new front end or a new tail end, but it can't change into two separate worms.

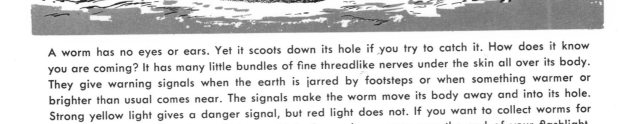

A worm has no eyes or ears. Yet it scoots down its hole if you try to catch it. How does it know you are coming? It has many little bundles of fine threadlike nerves under the skin all over its body. They give warning signals when the earth is jarred by footsteps or when something warmer or brighter than usual comes near. The signals make the worm move its body away and into its hole. Strong yellow light gives a danger signal, but red light does not. If you want to collect worms for fish bait at night, tie a piece of clear red plastic candy wrapper over the end of your flashlight.

WHY DO SOME DOGS HAVE MORE HAIR THAN OTHERS?

IN THE Far North, the only dogs that can live are those with lots of hair. Eskimo dogs have thick coats that keep them from freezing. But a thick-haired dog suffers in a hot country. In Mexico, where the weather gets hot, there is a dog that has almost no hair. It doesn't need any.

In between the Eskimo dog and the Mexican hairless are all kinds of dogs with all kinds of hair styles. Of course, they didn't choose the kind of hair they wear. People have done that. Long ago, men who liked hunting often raised only short-haired dogs. Furry coats got tangled in the brush in the woods.

Other men who raised dogs to run in races didn't like long hair, either. They thought that a dog could go faster if he didn't have to carry around a big load of heavy hair. But some people who raised dogs for pets liked the looks of a thick coat. Long-haired dogs now live in warm houses where they don't need a coat at all!

Asian Wild Horse

ARE THERE ANY WILD HORSES IN THE WORLD?

MORE THAN four hundred years ago, the Spaniards brought horses to America. Some of these horses escaped and ran wild. Others escaped from other pioneers later on. Little groups of runaways grew into large bands that used to roam all over the West. A few horses still escape and live in small bands in wilderness country, where people seldom go. But there is only one place in the world where there are wild horses whose ancestors have always been wild. That place is Mongolia, in Asia.

American Wild Horse

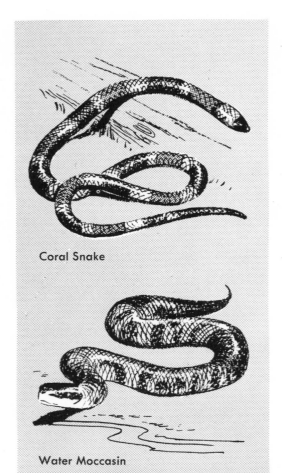

Coral Snake

Water Moccasin

SOME SNAKES eat other snakes, even poisonous ones. The poison does not do them any harm. Snakes can swallow things that are bigger around than they themselves are. This is possible because the jawbones are loosely attached, and the mouth can stretch to make room for a fat animal. The snake's slim body stretches to make space for the animal when it is inside.

Many snakes eat birds' eggs or frogs. Others eat insects, mice and other animals that destroy crops on farms. Because snakes do this valuable work, you should never kill one. It is too dangerous for you to try to kill a poisonous one. Leave that job to the experts.

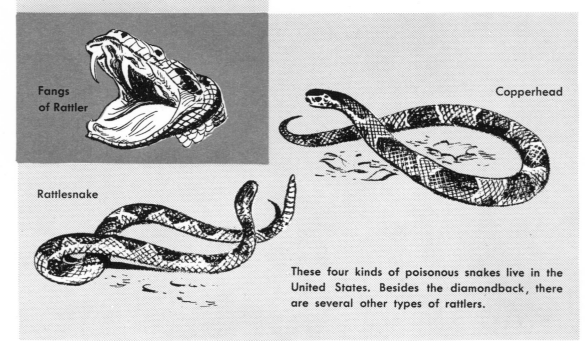

Fangs of Rattler

Copperhead

Rattlesnake

These four kinds of poisonous snakes live in the United States. Besides the diamondback, there are several other types of rattlers.

Ant's head
and feelers

WHAT ARE FEELERS FOR?

WATCH AN ANT hurrying along the ground. The two feelers on top of its head move this way and that. They tap the earth, the grass, anything in the way. If another ant comes by, the two may stop and touch each other with their busy feelers, which are also called antennae.

The ants seem to be picking up messages with their feelers, the way your TV antenna picks up a broadcast. The feelers are made in several sections, and each section is tuned to a different station! The section at the tip end detects the smell of an ant's own nest. The next section detects the odor of any other ant that has the same mother. The next one guides the ant back home by picking up a faint odor trail left by its own feet. Other sections of the antennae help ants to tell height and width when they are pulling food to the nest or lifting and carrying baby ants.

Many insects have antennae that detect odor clues. A male moth has been known to trace the odor of a mate for two miles. Bees find certain flowers by the odors that their antennae pick up. Other insects, such as mosquitoes, get certain sounds through their feelers. Still other insect antennae get information in ways that we don't yet understand completely. We do know that antennae are filled with material very much like the material in the insect's own brain.

HOW DO INSECTS KNOW WINTER IS COMING?

WHEN AUTUMN comes, many insects make some sort of winter home. The corn borer caterpillar chews a tunnel in a dry stalk or a corncob or a weed. It plugs the entrance with a substance from its own body and then takes a long rest.

Of course, a corn borer doesn't plan for cold weather the way people do. But some kind of signal makes it get ready for winter, even though the weather may still be warm. Scientists have raised the caterpillars in laboratories, and they have discovered what the signal is: nights that get longer and longer! If light is turned on in the laboratory, so that nights seem shorter, the caterpillars wake up, just as if spring had come. Each one cuts a round opening at the end of its tunnel and spins a silk curtain over the hole. About two weeks later the curtain is pushed aside, and out comes a creature with wings. The caterpillar has changed into a moth.

Other insects behave in a different way. When summer days are long, they lay eggs that hatch soon. But the same insects lay a different kind of egg when days get shorter. This kind of egg rests all winter and does not hatch until spring.

Scientists are still trying to find out just how darkness and light bring about these amazing changes in the way insects behave.

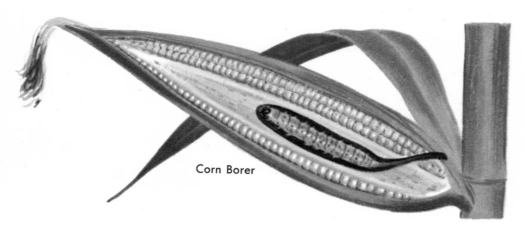

Corn Borer

Monarch Butterfly

Monarch butterflies go south for the winter, just as many birds do. In spring they fly back to their summer homes again. People in Canada have glued tiny tags onto the wings of thousands of monarchs. In winter, other people have found the tagged butterflies as far away as Texas. And some that make the long round trip turn up with their tags in Canada again the next year!

HOW DOES A MEASURING WORM MEASURE?

A MEASURING WORM is not a worm, and it doesn't measure anything. But it has a way of walking, all its own, and it does look as if it is marking off distance, inch by inch. Some people call it an inchworm. First it stretches out its body as much as it can. Next it braces its front legs and pulls its hind legs forward, making its body go up into a loop. (Some people also call it a looper.) Then it reaches its front legs out again, pulls its hind legs up, and so on.

A measuring worm is a caterpillar that will later turn into a moth. Most caterpillars have two whole rows of legs, all the way along their undersides. But the measuring worm only has the ones in front and rear. As a rule, its body is colored greenish brown, and this helps it to escape its enemies. When it grabs onto a branch with its hind legs, and stretches itself straight out, it looks almost exactly like a tiny green twig. This fools many a bird that is looking for a juicy worm to eat.

WHY DO BEES BUZZ?

WHEN A BEE comes buzzing, we usually get out of its way. We have learned that bees can sting. But the buzzing itself is only the sound made by the bee's wings.

Sometimes bees buzz when they are not flying. Two groups of them gather inside the hive where they live. One group stays on the right side of the entrance, and the other group stays on the left side. All of them fan the air with their wings. The wings on one side bring air into the hive where it picks up heat and moisture. The wings on the other side drive the hot, moist air out. When you hear the low buzz of bees inside the hive, you can tell they are working their cooling system.

HOW DO WORMS DIG HOLES IN THE GROUND?

EARTHWORMS make holes by eating their way through the ground! A worm's food is all mixed up with the soil — such things as bits of dead leaves or roots or small bugs. When a worm eats, it digs itself a home at the same time.

After a worm has taken in all it can hold, it comes back to the surface and empties the earth and waste material outside. Then it goes back underground. It can move along quite fast with the help of tiny stiff bristles on its underside.

In spring, after a warm rain, great numbers of worms come up out of their holes and get fresh leaves to eat. Robins are often waiting to grab them. If a worm gets part way back into its hole, it anchors its stiff little bristles in the soil. The robin and the worm may have quite a tug of war before the worm gives up.

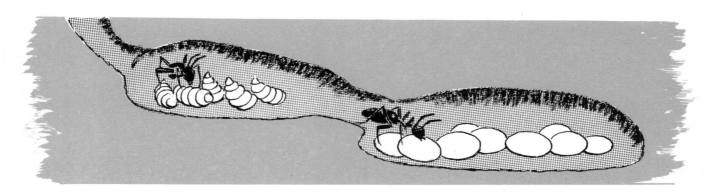

ARE FLYING ANTS THE SAME AS ANTS THAT CRAWL?

THE ANTS we usually see scurrying around on the ground are worker ants. They build the nest where an ant colony lives. They get the food for the whole colony. They care for the baby ants that hatch out of eggs in underground tunnels. But workers don't lay eggs, and they can't fly. They have no wings.

A queen ant does all the egg-laying in a colony. And for a short while, before she starts to lay, she *does* have wings. So do male ants. The queen mates with a male while both of them are flying. During the mating season, they are flying ants. After she has mated, the queen ant comes down to earth and never flies again. She actually bites off her wings, and then she starts a new colony where she spends all her time underground laying eggs. She may keep on doing this for ten years. Workers and males live only for a short time, but as long as an ant hill has a queen that once had wings, it can keep on going.

WHY DO MOSQUITO BITES ITCH?

SOME LUCKY people do not get itching bumps when mosquitoes bite them. Most of us do. Doctors believe that these bumps and itches are signs of an allergy. We are allergic to something the mosquitoes leave under our skin.

It is only the female mosquito that bites. She makes a prick with her sharp beak. Then she pokes her hollow mouth-tube down and sucks out a drop or two of blood. This is her way of getting food. She gets it easily, because the blood does not form a clot the way it does soon after you prick yourself with a pin. A liquid in the mosquito's mouth keeps the blood from clotting. Most people are allergic to this liquid. Wherever a tiny bit of it is left under your skin, the skin swells up and begins to itch.

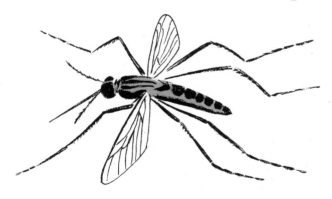

Female mosquitoes bite people and animals. The males live on plant juices. If you catch a mosquito with wide, feathery feelers on its head, you can be sure it is a male and it won't bite. If you hear a mosquito singing, you do not need to catch it in order to find out if it is a biter. It is! Only the females make this loud whining song.

67

WHY DOES A JET PLANE LEAVE A TRAIL IN THE SKY?

VERY OFTEN after a jet plane has gone out of sight, you can see the white streaks it leaves behind in the sky. The streaks are called vapor trails, and they appear when the plane flies at just the right speed through air that has just the right amount of moisture in it.

There is always some moisture in the air, although the particles of water are so small that you can't see them. When many particles gather together into little drops, they form a cloud. A vapor trail is a cloud that forms in special whirlpools of air behind the tip ends of the wings of a fast-moving plane. The whirling air expands, and as it does so, it cools off. This sudden cooling makes the invisible bits of moisture draw together into a visible cloud — a vapor trail. When the moisture has cooled a great deal, the vapor trail may be made up of tiny particles of ice.

Sometimes you see trails behind each of a plane's jet engines. These are not quite the same, although they are made of water, too. When fuel burns in an engine, steam is formed along with other gases. The gases rush out behind the plane in great, hot streams. The cooler outside air turns the moisture into a ribbon of cloud, just as steam from a teakettle becomes cloudy as it cools down a little way from the spout.

A whale makes a kind of vapor trail when it comes up to blow! People used to think a whale blew a spray of sea water into the air. We know now that it blows out a huge jet of moist breath that turns cloudy when it is cooled in the air outside the whale's warm body.

WHAT ARE G-FORCES?

PERHAPS you have taken a ride in a very fast elevator. When it first starts, you feel as if your insides are being pulled downward. Your whole body seems to be extra heavy, as if you weighed more than usual. The same thing happens to an airplane pilot when he takes off very fast. If his plane keeps on going at greater and greater speed, he feels heavier and heavier. His body acts as if it weighs more. It actually does.

This feeling of extra weight disappears as soon as the plane travels at an even speed, no matter what that speed is. But now suppose the plane suddenly slows down and comes to a very quick stop. Again the pilot will feel heavy, as if a great force is pressing on him. Both times it is the change in speed that has the effect of increasing his weight. The force that acts on him is called a G-force.

One G-force is equal to the ordinary pull of earth's gravity on your body. A force of 2 G's has the effect of doubling the pull of gravity, which means doubling your weight. Four or 5 G's will make you feel uncomfortable, but fliers and astronauts are able to stand 10 G's or more for short periods of time.

This machine, called a centrifuge, can be whirled around and around. A pilot rides in a cabin at the end of the long whirling arm. As he goes faster and faster, he feels the same G-forces that he feels when an airplane or a space capsule increases its speed. The centrifuge helps experimenters to find out exactly what G-forces do and how to keep them from harming the pilot's body.

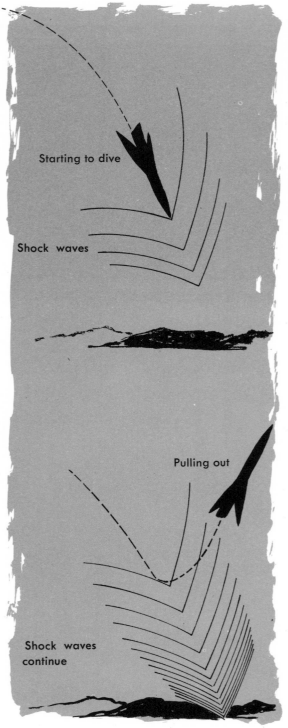

Starting to dive

Shock waves

Pulling out

Shock waves
continue

A SOUND is made by invisible ripples in the air. If you could see them, the ripples would look something like the little waves made by a rock dropped in water. Sound waves travel very fast — as much as 760 miles an hour — and they spread out well ahead of ordinary airplanes. But what happens when a plane goes so swiftly that it catches up with the sound waves? There is no chance for ripples to form. The plane simply pushes air ahead of it the way a snow plow pushes snow.

In the days before very speedy planes were built, fliers used to worry about going faster than sound. Perhaps the air would be squeezed together into a sort of wall or barrier. People talked about such a wall and called it the "sound barrier." They thought a plane might be damaged by trying to fly through it.

At last a plane with special wings and body shape did fly faster than sound. The pilot felt some shaking and rocking. Then the air seemed to get beautifully still and smooth! The sound barrier *could* be crossed.

The air ahead of a plane flying faster than sound is pressed into a cone-shaped layer called a *shock wave*. When a plane heads downward at such speed, the shock wave moves on until it hits the earth. The explosive noise it makes is called a *sonic boom*. Powerful shock waves often break windows.

When a supersonic plane flies straight and level, its shock waves cause a constant boom that follows it along the ground.

WHAT IS THE SOUND BARRIER?

WHEN YOU hear an airplane flying overhead, your ears tell your brain and your brain tells your eyes where to look for it. If the sound comes from behind you, then you turn around, and as a rule, you can locate the plane in the sky behind you. The sounds of its propeller and engine have traveled out ahead of the plane itself.

But sometimes when you look for a plane in the sky, you can't locate it. Your eyes search where your ears tell you there should be a plane, but it isn't there. This plane has been traveling faster than the noise it makes. By the time the noise reaches your ears, the plane is already in a different part of the sky. It may be out of sight before you can locate it. It is going faster than the speed of sound and it is called a supersonic plane.

When a pilot is traveling at exactly the speed of sound, he says he is traveling at Mach 1. At Mach 2, he is traveling twice as fast as sound. But if you ask him how many miles an hour he is going, he will answer, "That depends." The speed of sound varies. At sea level, it travels about 760 miles an hour. But high above the earth the air is much thinner, and sound travels more slowly in thin air. At high altitudes, Mach 1 may be as slow as 660 miles an hour, and Mach 2 is then 1,320 miles an hour.

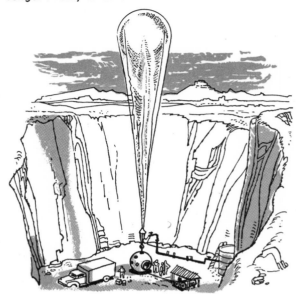

Helium gas in a large balloon has lifted a passenger twenty miles above the earth.

WHERE DOES A LOST BALLOON GO?

A TOY BALLOON floats up and away if you let go of the string. Will it keep on going forever, all the way out into space? No, it will stop rising after a while. Winds that blow above the earth will carry it along high in the air. Then gradually the gas that lifted the balloon will leak out. Even though the opening is tied very tight, the gas can push its way out, bit by bit, right through the rubber itself. Finally the balloon will begin to come down, until at last it falls to the ground.

Sometimes people do an experiment with balloons. They fasten postcards to the strings. A message on each one asks anybody who finds the card to return it, along with his name and address. Of course, most of the balloons come down where no one sees them — in lakes or woods or weed patches. But once in a while the senders do get cards back from places a hundred miles or more away.

What about the gas that leaked out of the balloon? Does it go on pushing its way up and up forever? If it is a gas called helium, some of it will do just that. Some particles of the gas will fly upward as fast as rockets. The pull of gravity cannot hold these back, and away they go — out into space.

72

WHAT IS THIN AIR?

AIR IS a mixture of invisible things called gases. A gas is made of particles so small that you can't see them — smaller even than specks of dust. These particles, called molecules, are very light, and they move around constantly, hitting each other and bouncing away.

Even though gas molecules are tiny, they do have weight. They surround the earth in an airy blanket many miles thick. Gravity pulls on them, just as it pulls on everything else, and close to the earth's surface the bouncing molecules are squeezed in by all the other molecules above them.

But suppose you climb a mountain that is five thousand feet high. Gravity still pulls on the molecules, although not so strongly. That is one of the rules about gravity — the farther you go above the earth, the weaker its pull becomes. Also, when you are on the five-thousand-foot mountain, almost a mile of the air blanket now lies below you. Up here the molecules can bounce around more easily. They have more freedom to spread out, with space between. And so we say the air is thinner. Thin air is something like thin hair. There are bald spots.

Airplanes can fly ten miles or more above the earth. But people who go that high can't get as much oxygen as they need from the thin air. Sometimes a pilot wears a special helmet attached to a tank of oxygen. A passenger plane has machinery that pulls in the thin air, squeezes it together, and pumps it into the cabin for passengers to breathe.

In South America there are towns and farms on mountainsides more than three miles high. The people who live and work in the thin air have extra big chests, so that they can get an extra amount of air in their lungs.

WHAT IS THE DIFFERENCE BETWEEN AIR AND OXYGEN?

SOMETIMES you hear this: "We must have *air* to breathe." Sometimes you hear: "We must have *oxygen* to breathe."

Which is right? Both are right.

Air is a mixture of several different gases, and one of them is oxygen.

When you breathe air, you take oxygen into your lungs, although it is mixed with other gases, too.

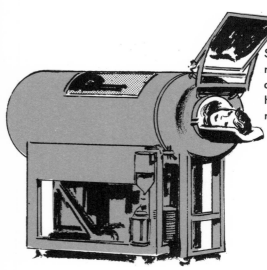

Sometimes when people are sick, their lungs need help with the job of pumping air. A wonderful machine called an iron lung gives this help. It has a bed inside so that a patient can rest while the machine is at work.

A man in a diving suit under the water breathes air that comes through a long hose from an air pump on his ship.

WHY DOESN'T OUR BREATHING USE UP ALL THE OXYGEN IN THE AIR?

PEOPLE and other animals do use a great deal of oxygen. We breathe it into our lungs, and in our bodies it combines with other chemicals. One of these is called carbon. When oxygen combines with carbon in a certain way, a new gas is formed. The gas is carbon dioxide, and it leaves our lungs when we breathe out.

It happens that plants need the very gas that we and other animals breathe out. The leaves of growing plants take in carbon dioxide. They use the carbon from this combination and send pure oxygen out into the air. Plants keep on making new oxygen for animals, and animals keep on making new carbon dioxide for plants.

WHAT MAKES THE WIND BLOW?

THE SUN can make the wind blow! The faraway sun can make air move across the earth in a wind.

First, sunshine heats the earth. Then the earth heats the air that is close to it. As the air gets warmer, it also gets lighter. Up it goes, while cooler air moves in to take its place. This is the kind of motion you can see in a turning wheel — as one part is going up, another part is moving along the ground.

High above the earth, the warm air grows cool, and down it comes again. Once more the earth warms it. Again it rises, and the great wheel of air keeps turning.

You can feel it turning on a hot day at the seashore or beside a lake. The earth soaks up more heat from the sun than the water does. This means that the air above the earth grows warm and light, while the air above the water stays cool. The warm, light air rises. Offshore, the cooler air begins to move. It flows in over the land to take the warm air's place. That is why you are likely to have a cool breeze at the shore on a sunshiny day.

Some winds are caused by the spinning of the earth itself.

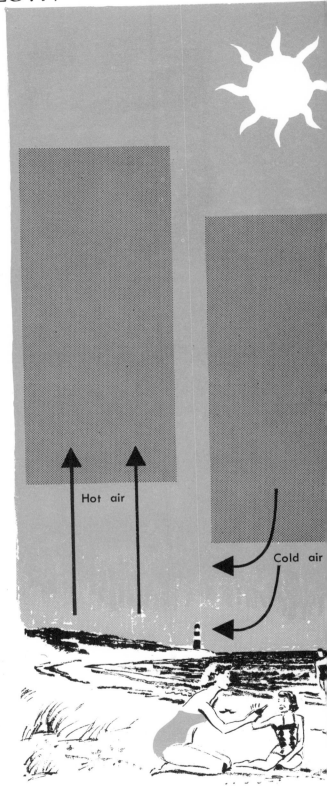

Hot air

Cold air

WHAT IS THE JET STREAM?

SEVERAL miles over our heads there is a great, swift wind that blows steadily, day and night, even when the air around us is quite still. Pilots discovered this river of air when they first began to cross the country in fast, high-flying planes. They called it the jet stream, and when it was going their way, their planes could ride along in it as boats ride downstream with the current of a river. Weather men have now discovered other tremendous wind streams high above the earth. Although we can't feel the jet stream winds blowing down here, our weather can be greatly changed by them as they swoop along far above the clouds.

WHAT IS A MIRAGE?

ON A HOT DAY you have probably seen what looked like a pool of water ahead of you in the road. If you watched carefully you noticed that this pool moved as you moved. You could never catch up with it. It wasn't water at all. It was a mirage. Something looked like water, but it was actually a reflection in a mirror — a reflection of light from the sky.

This kind of mirror is made of air, not glass, and it only appears when the temperature is right. First, there must be a layer of hot air over the pavement. At the same time there must be a layer of cool air just above the hot air. Now rays of light go in a straight line through cool air, but a curious thing happens when they hit the hot air. They bend upward. Light from the sky comes down, bends, then goes on to your eyes. So you see a reflection of the sky, which looks like clear water, and you don't see the surface of the road at all.

If you ever visit a desert, you may see this same kind of mirage. Instead of hot dry sand in front of you, a beautiful lake may appear. There are other kinds of mirages, too. When the air near the ground is cold, and a warm layer lies above it, the air-mirror works the opposite way. Light rays from something on the earth go up, then bend back downward. In this kind of mirage you can see the reflection of houses or ships or other things that are out of sight many miles away. Mirages like this — and other kinds, too — sometimes happen in the Arctic.

Although the things you see in a mirage really aren't where they seem to be, you can take photographs of them! That is, you can photograph the reflection you see, just as someone can take a picture of your reflection in a mirror.

Mirages have many forms. Sometimes you see objects upside down because of the way the air-mirror works. Occasionally the layers of air make two different mirrors that give two different reflections of the same thing.

Three ways of launching a glider.

Otto Lilienthal built and flew this glider before the Wright brothers flew their first plane.

HOW DOES A GLIDER FLY?

A GLIDER has no engine, but it flies for the same reason that an airplane flies. Its wings are shaped in just the right way to lift it as it moves through the air. It has large wings and a light body, and it does not need to move as fast as a heavy plane. So a glider pilot can use the slower motion of air currents to keep his wings lifting.

The pilot knows that warm air rises. Currents of warm air rise in different places at different times of day, and the pilot knows where to find them.

If a rising current is big enough, he can ride it. He turns this way and that and hunts for every strong draft within the current which will carry him still farther up. Or he may take a sort of roller-coaster ride, down from the top of a warm current and across a patch of cool air. The fast down-glide gives him a head start into a second rising current which then carries him aloft once more.

Gliders are used mostly for fun now, but they are important for another reason. People learned how to fly gliders, and then they were able to invent airplanes with engines.

WHEN YOU rub two things against each other, you make them warmer. Most things don't burn when you rub them, but matches are different. There are chemicals in the head of an ordinary wooden match. Heat or a sharp blow will make them burst into flame. The flame then heats the wood in the match, and the wood burns, too.

Some matches will burn only if you scratch them against a special strip of paper on their own package. This strip has one kind of chemical in it. The heads of the matches have another kind. When you press the two together, they mix and make a small, hot explosion. The heat starts the flame. As long as the two chemicals are separated, they cannot light up accidentally, and so these matches are called safety matches.

Wet matches will not light because the moisture keeps them cool. They cannot get hot enough to burst into flame.

WHY DO WE GREASE A FRYING PAN?

GREASE keeps food from sticking to a pan. Cooks knew this for hundreds of years, but they had no idea why it happened. Now scientists have discovered that the grease and metal pull toward each other. The pulling makes a layer of grease cling to the pan. This slippery grease layer stays between the hot metal and the food. After an egg or a pancake or a fish is cooked it slides out of the pan without sticking.

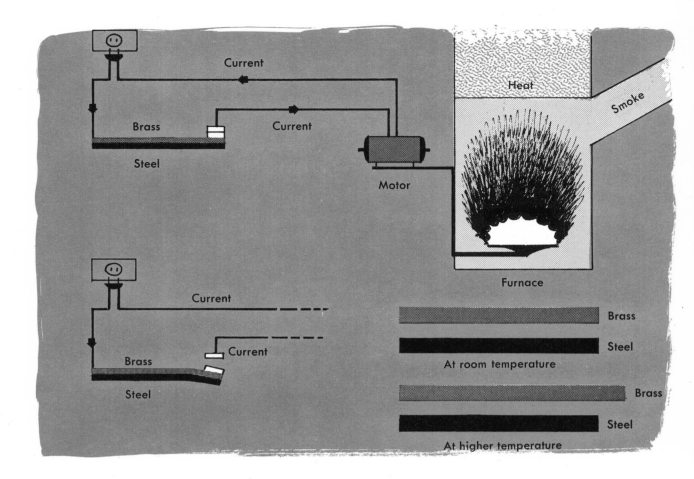

HOW DOES A THERMOSTAT WORK?

PERHAPS your house has an oil or gas heater that goes on and off all by itself. If the house gets cold, the heat goes on. When it is warm again, the fire stops burning until the house cools down once more. The automatic switch that starts and stops the furnace is called a thermostat.

The pictures show one kind of thermostat. It is connected with an electric motor which runs a heater. In the first picture, the electricity is turned on, and the heater is going. In the second picture the electricity has been switched off. There is a space between the two little square parts of the switch. How did the space get there?

Before we can answer that question, we have to know something about the two long, thin strips marked *brass* and *steel* which are fastened tightly together so that they can't slip apart. Anything made of brass or steel gets a little bigger when it is heated and smaller when it is cooled. It expands and contracts. When heated, brass expands more than steel does.

80

Now let's see what happens to the strips of brass and steel when the room grows warm. Both of them expand. If they were separate strips, the brass would stretch out a little beyond the end of the steel. But they are tightly joined, and so the expanding brass strip forces the steel to bend downward. This opens the switch, and electric current cannot get across the empty space. The motor stops running. The heater goes off.

When the room grows colder, the two metal strips become smaller. They straighten out, and the switch closes. Again current flows to the motor and the heater is turned on.

Making ice cream long ago

The ice cream man uses dry ice

WHAT IS DRY ICE?

DRY ICE is cold, and it comes in a solid white lump. But watch what happens to it in a warm room. It doesn't melt and become a liquid as ordinary ice does. It simply disappears. How can a chunk of solid material vanish without a trace? The mystery clears up when you discover that the material doesn't really vanish. It turns into an invisible gas that mixes with the air of the room.

Dry ice is a frozen form of a gas called carbon dioxide. There are always some particles of carbon dioxide in the air. You can't see them because they are so small and widely scattered. But if you cool the gas very, very much, the particles draw together and make a solid mass.

Dry ice is a great deal colder than ice made from water. This means you have to be careful with it. It will give you a dangerous frostbite if you hold it in your hand for more than a few moments.

AN AQUALUNG is an invention that allows you to breathe while you are swimming under water. Instead of coming up for air every half-minute or so, you carry air in a tank on your back and breathe it through a tube attached to a mask over your face. A very small tank can hold a lot of air — enough to keep you swimming for many minutes. The secret is this: Air can be pressed and squeezed until it takes up much less space than before. *Compressed air* is the name for it.

An aqualung's tank of compressed air has a small faucet called a valve which lets air flow through the tube to the mask. The valve is made so that it automatically lets the swimmer get just exactly the amount of air he needs for breathing under water.

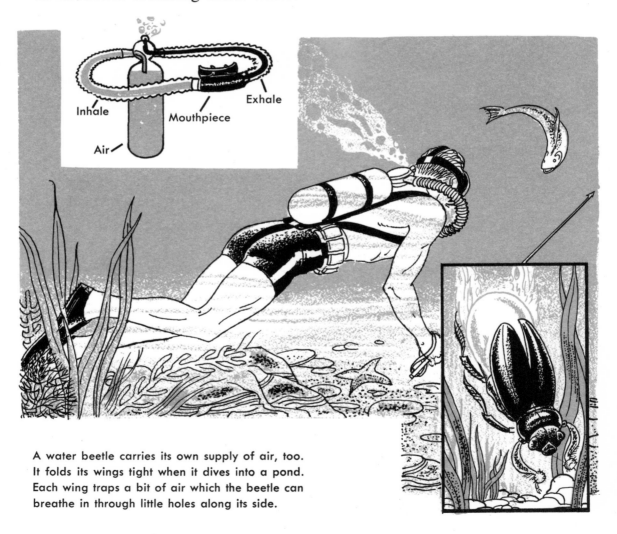

Inhale

Exhale

Mouthpiece

Air

A water beetle carries its own supply of air, too. It folds its wings tight when it dives into a pond. Each wing traps a bit of air which the beetle can breathe in through little holes along its side.

The Savannah

Atomic energy runs this ship. Less than 150 pounds of atomic fuel will keep it sailing for three years. An ordinary ship's engines use up thousands of pounds of fuel oil every month.

WHAT IS A REACTOR?

A REACTOR is a well-behaved relative of an atomic bomb. If a bomb explodes, it lets loose in one big burst vast quantities of heat energy and light and X-rays and other powerful rays. In a reactor the same amounts and kinds of energy are released, but they are let loose slowly and evenly enough so that they can do useful work. Atomic energy can make steam to run an electric power plant or a ship. The rays that are dangerous in an atomic bomb can now be put to work making materials for doctors to use when they study and cure diseases.

Scientists sometimes draw atoms like this

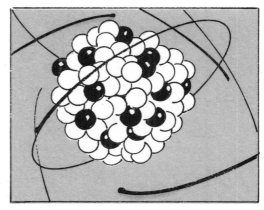

The inside of a reactor looks something like this

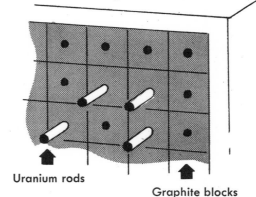

Uranium rods

Graphite blocks

WHAT MAKES YOUR SHOES SQUEAK?

IF YOUR shoes squeak when you walk, they probably have leather soles. The sound is made by two layers of rough leather rubbing against each other. Soles aren't so noisy if they have a third layer of smooth material, like a sandwich filling, between the two rough ones.

Have you ever heard a horse's saddle squeak? It, too, has layers of leather that rub together.

WHY DO TELEPHONE WIRES HUM?

TELEPHONE wires often make a humming sound. The hum is caused by the wind, not by people talking or singing over the phone. When the wind blows against the wires, they move back and forth. Their quick, regular motion is somewhat like the vibrating of a banjo string. If the wires are strung tightly between telephone poles, they make an almost musical sound. The same wires may give different sounds on different days, because changes in the speed and direction of the wind will make them vibrate in different ways.

Electric wires on high poles outdoors sometimes hum, but for a different reason. They vibrate because of sudden changes in the flow of electricity that goes through them.

LONG AGO soldiers called knights wore metal armor over their bodies and heads. Their faces were protected by movable metal flaps called visors. When two knights met, they had to raise their visors to see whether they were enemies or friends. The motion of lifting the flap became a habit that stayed with fighting men after they stopped wearing the metal visors. That is how the soldiers' salute got started.

WHY CAN YOU BEND A TIN BOX BUT NOT A GLASS BOTTLE?

YOU PROBABLY know that everything in the world is made of tiny bits of material called atoms. A tin box is made of atoms that belong to a group of substances called metals. Each atom pulls on its neighbors as if it were a little magnet, and scientists believe that they are all stacked and packed together tightly in a kind of pattern. But the pattern is not quite perfect, and in the places where it is not, the atoms can slip past each other when you put pressure on them. Although they slip, they don't lose their pull on each other. And so the metal bends but does not break.

The atoms that make up glass also pull on each other. They, too, are packed together closely, but not in any orderly pattern. When you put pressure on them, they don't slip. They hold tight until the pressure or a blow is too much for them. And then they suddenly give up altogether. That is when the glass breaks.

If you heat glass slowly till it is very, very hot, some but not all of the atoms loosen their grip. Then the glass will bend.

85

WHERE DID LIVING THINGS COME FROM?

ONCE there was absolutely nothing to see anywhere on the surface of the earth except water and bare, jagged rock. Not a single plant lived on the land or in the sea. There were no animals or people because they couldn't have found any food to eat.

But important things were happening. Lightning flashed. Volcanoes exploded. And it rained and rained and rained. The endless cloudbursts wore down the rocks, and many chemicals from the rocks were washed into the warm water of the oceans.

Some of these chemicals that sloshed around in sea water had a way of combining with certain others. One in particular was a great joiner. Its name was carbon.

Hundreds and hundreds of different carbon combinations formed. Often the combinations broke up very quickly. But sometimes they did cling together for a while. They formed tiny blobs, and at last some of the blobs started to act in a very special way. When they broke up, they always broke into twin parts, exactly alike. Then each part gathered up more chemicals which arranged themselves in exactly the right way to make another pair of twins. These carbon-mixture twins could go on and on making other droplets just like themselves.

Some of the twin-makers joined still other blobs of many kinds. In all of this mixing around, more and more different chemical combinations were formed. One of them was green, and it happened to have a special power. It put sunlight to work making the things we call starch and sugar. Food had appeared in the world. We call the green substance chlorophyll, and the droplets that had it were the first green plants.

With food in the warm, soupy sea, many different blobs could grow and change in many ways. Some began to absorb the tiny green plants. This was a kind of eating. Very small animals had now appeared in the world. These first plants and animals grew and changed into new kinds. And these changes led to all the different kinds of plants and animals in the world today. *Evolution* is the name that scientists give to this kind of change.

Nobody was there to see the first plants and animals, a few billion years ago. We have to use clues that help us figure out what must have gone on. Most scientists agree that the beginning was very slow. It probably didn't happen all at once with some kind of big bang, although lightning may have started some of the first chemical combinations.

Many scientists are so sure of their clues that they are trying to create living things in laboratories. Already they have made some of the most important carbon combinations. Perhaps if they keep on they can really show how things started so long ago.

DO THEY PUT REAL GOLD ON THE TOPS OF BUILDINGS?

THE BUILDINGS where State Legislatures meet very often have domes covered with real gold. So do many other buildings. Gold is so expensive that it seems strange to use it on a roof. But the fact is that a little gold can be stretched to cover a very big surface. When it is carefully beaten with a hammer, gold spreads out into a thin sheet which is called a leaf. A lump of gold that weighs less than two packages of chewing gum can be beaten into enough gold leaf to cover a football field!

WHY DOES A WHIP CRACK?

WHEN YOU swing a whip, it pushes air ahead of it. The push is greatest at the tip, which moves much faster than the handle you are holding. If you swing the whip hard, the tip presses very hard against the air and squeezes it together. Then, if you jerk the whip, the tip goes even faster and slaps still harder against the air ahead of it. This sudden squeezing of the air makes sound waves that travel quickly. When they reach your ears, you hear a sharp crack.

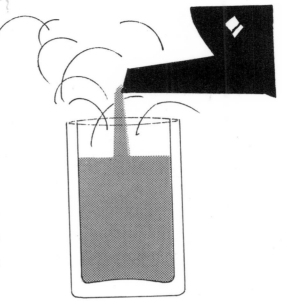

MOST THINGS get a little bigger when they are heated. If you put a glass into a pan of water and warm it slowly, all the parts of the glass expand evenly. The whole thing gets a little bigger. But suppose you pour boiling water into a cold glass. The inside expands quickly, while the outside stays the same size. The pressure from inside is so strong and sudden that the whole glass breaks.

WHAT MAKES A BASEBALL CURVE?

WHAT HAPPENS when a pitcher throws a curve? He makes the ball spin round and round, while at the same time it is travelling toward the batter. As the ball spins, it whirls air along with it. This whirling makes the air press a little harder on one side than on the other. If there is less pressure on the left side, the ball curves very slightly to the left.

A curve ball usually fools the batter's eyes. It seems to make a sudden wide swerve as it comes over the plate. Photographs have showed that the ball does not make a sharp break away from the plate. The break is called an optical illusion. This means that the batter's eyes just fail to see the path of the ball accurately.

Here is another optical illusion that you can test. Are the two horizontal lines straight or curving?

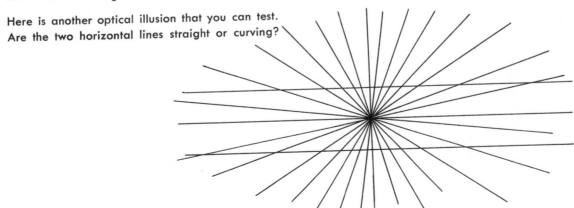

WHY ARE WORDS SPELLED IN SUCH MIXED-UP WAYS?

THE PEOPLE who lived in England long ago had a language that they spoke, but they did not write it or read it. Those who lived in the western part of the country and those who lived in the eastern part did not always pronounce their words in the same ways. This is true in our country, too. Some people in the West say *idea* and *butter,* but when some people in Boston use the same words, they say *idear* and *buttah.*

You can guess what happened when writing finally came to England. Each person spelled words the way he pronounced them. Spelling got still more mixed up after England was conquered by people called Normans who had a different language and their own way of writing down sounds. All of this happened before the invention of printing. At that time, books had to be copied by hand. Each man who copied a book spelled as he pleased, and nobody cared so long as the meaning was clear.

The first book printers began to use regular ways of spelling some words, and the people who wrote the books thought this was a good idea. Still, if a printer wanted to make a line come out even so that the page would look neat, he might add or subtract a letter here and there. For example, he would use *knowe* or *kenowe* or *know.*

The men who made dictionaries picked and chose the spellings they liked. At last, about two hundred years ago, almost all dictionary makers and teachers and printers began to agree on some rules. There seems to be no reason why they kept some of the odd and unreasonable spellings. Perhaps they hated to change old habits. Perhaps they just liked the way the words looked.

thepeoplewholivedinenglandlongagohadalanguagethattheyspok

ebuttheydidnotwriteitorreaditthosewholivedinthewesternpar

tofthecountryandthosewholivedintheeasternpartdidnotalways

Long ago writers did not use any periods or commas or question marks or any other punctuation marks. They did not even separate one word from another. Whole strings of letters just went on and on. Then printers began to divide up words. They used punctuation marks, and they were the ones who gave us pages that are easy to read.

A STAMP is just a piece of paper with a picture and some words printed on one side and some glue on the other side. What makes one of these bits of paper worth any money at all? What makes a four-cent stamp worth four cents?

When you buy a stamp, you also buy work from the post-office. You get a letter delivered. After the stamp has done its job, the post-office says it is worthless. You must buy a new one for each letter you send.

But people often pay money for stamps that have already been used. Collectors have fun just trying to collect many different kinds. Certain kinds are hard to find. To get one of these rare stamps some collectors are willing to pay a great deal of money. They *think* it is worth something, and that is what gives it value. If you collect stamps because they are especially beautiful or tell an interesting story or show all kinds of animals, then those are the ones that have value to you.

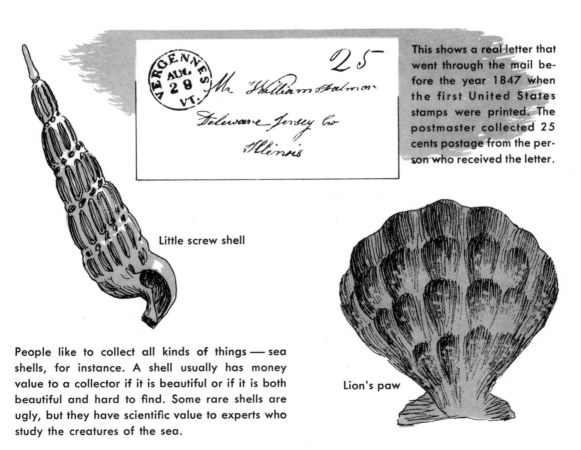

This shows a real letter that went through the mail before the year 1847 when the first United States stamps were printed. The postmaster collected 25 cents postage from the person who received the letter.

Little screw shell

Lion's paw

People like to collect all kinds of things — sea shells, for instance. A shell usually has money value to a collector if it is beautiful or if it is both beautiful and hard to find. Some rare shells are ugly, but they have scientific value to experts who study the creatures of the sea.

LONG, LONG AGO people found that they needed to count. Suppose a hunter saw one deer and six lions. He could tell his friends simply, "Deer — lion." But they might think he meant one deer, one lion, and this could turn out to be a sad mistake!

There are still people in the world who live as the ancient hunters lived. Some of them have words for *one, two, three*, and everything above three is called *many*. This is good enough to save a man's friends from lions. But it did not work very well when a skilful hunter wanted to trade an extra buffalo skin for six stone knives. He needed to show exactly six. He and other people began doing just what you would do. They used their fingers. When they used all ten fingers, they got into the habit of counting by tens.

This way of counting seems natural to us, but it is not the only way. Some people used their toes as well as their fingers. They counted by twenties. Others counted up to three on the joints of a finger.

After people discovered how to raise grain, farmers grew more food than they could eat. They exchanged some of this extra food for things they wanted, and they paid some of it to kings or priests for taxes. Farmers and rulers needed large numbers to keep track of all the food that was traded or brought to the tax storehouse. If a man didn't bring all that the ruler wanted, the tax collector had to figure out how much the man still owed. Farmers also needed to count days, so that they could plant seeds at the same time each year. All this measuring and counting of things and food and days was the beginning of arithmetic.

Written numbers were used in most countries where powerful rulers wanted to know just how much wealth they had. But in Peru, the Inca Indians kept their records with knots tied in strings of different colors. The special bundle of strings they used was called a *quipu*.

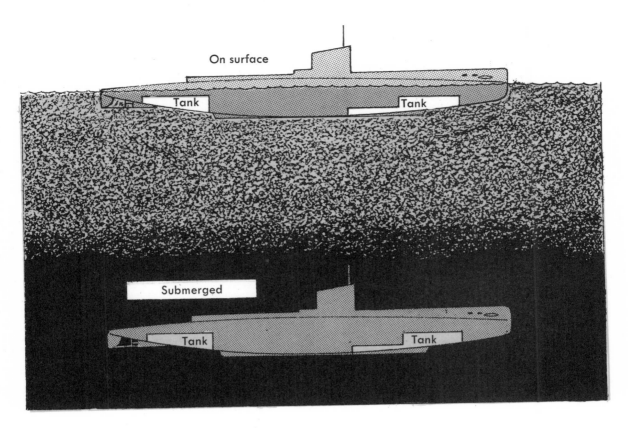

On surface

Tank   Tank

Submerged

Tank   Tank

HOW DOES A SUBMARINE GO UP AND DOWN?

A SUBMARINE is a ship that can travel both under water and on the surface of the ocean. It has several huge tanks that contain nothing but air while it is on the surface. In the bottom of each tank is a kind of door called a valve. When this valve is opened, water pours in, fills the tank and pushes air out through another valve in the top. As the tanks fill with water, the submarine sinks below the surface.

When it is time to bring the sub back up, the captain orders the tanks to be emptied. Pumps force the water out of the tanks while air is blown in. Where does the air come from? It is carried along, squeezed and pressed into huge metal bottles called flasks. When a flask is opened, the compressed air rushes into the tank and pushes the water out. With its tanks full of air, which is lighter than water, the submarine rises to the surface.

A sub has small stubby fins called diving planes. These diving planes act like the wings on an airplane. They can hold the sub steady or make it climb or dive.

HOW CAN YOU DO ARITHMETIC WITH ROMAN NUMERALS?

THE ROMAN numerals look as if they would be very hard to work with. But it is fun to use them in simple problems like these:

Add		*Subtract*	
CL XV I	(166)	L X X V I I	(77)
X I I	(12)	X I	(11)
CL X XV I II	(178)	L X V I	(66)

But suppose you had to work with a bigger number — for instance, CCCCLXXXXVIII, which in our numerals is 498. It is hard to keep track of such long figures, and instead of writing them out, the Romans used a very ancient kind of adding machine called an abacus. Storekeepers and business men in Rome usually had slaves who worked the abacus and did the figuring for them.

94

WHAT IS THE LAST NUMBER?

Suppose you were to start counting and did nothing but count, day and night, for the rest of your life. Would you get to the last number? The answer is no, because there is no last number. People who study mathematics tell us that we can never get to the end of numbers by counting. No matter how big a number we think of, there is always a bigger number. This idea is a very important one in science, and it has a name — the idea of infinity. Scientists write infinity this way: ∞

A million is a large number. A billion is larger. From there on, we don't very often use names for numbers, and some of them don't even have names. The largest number that has a name is a *googol*. It is a 1 with 100 zeros after it.

$10,000,000,000,000,000,000,000,000,000,000,000,000,
000,000,000,000,000,000,000,000,000,000,000,
000,000,000,000,000,000,000,000,000.

One day a nine-year-old boy was talking with his uncle who taught mathematics in a college. The uncle showed the boy a very large number — 1 followed by 100 zeros — and asked what it should be called. "A googol," the boy answered, and that is the true story of how a googol got its name.

95

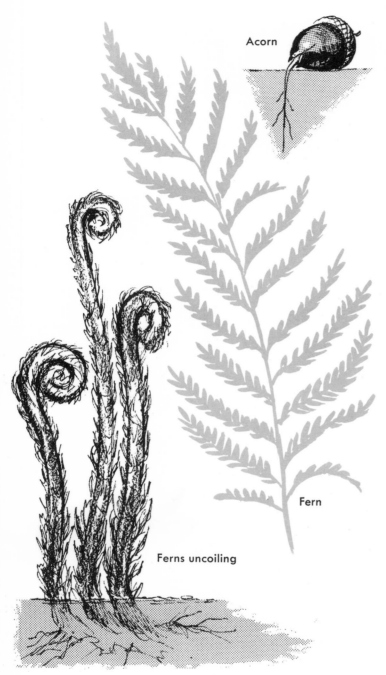

Acorn

Fern

Ferns uncoiling

THE GROWING tip of a root seems much too soft and fragile for the job it has to do. It must work its way through rough earth, over sharp-edged rocks. It often has to force a path through clay that seems as hard as stone.

The secret is in little sacks called cells which form as the root grows. Each cell has a thin but strong covering, and it is filled with liquid, mostly water. One by one, the cells of a growing root fill up. A cell all by itself may not seem very strong. But a root is made of thousands and thousands of cells. When all of them together press against the earth, they can work a hole in it. Growing roots can shove sideways, too. If a root enters a crack in a rock, it can break the rock apart! Root tips have special cells that wear away, leaving a slippery juice that helps the root to slide along.

Plants often push their way upward through frozen earth or through pavement several inches thick. They, too, get strength from the pressure of growing cells. The best pushers are those which start their growth curled around into a coil. A coil unwinding is like a man shoving a weight upward on his strong shoulders.

96

WHY DO LEAVES TURN DIFFERENT COLORS IN AUTUMN?

THE GREEN that you see in leaves all summer comes from a chemical called a pigment. Leaves also have a yellow pigment that you can't see because the green hides it. In autumn, the leaves stop making green pigment, and then you *can* see the yellow.

Autumn leaves can also have red, orange or purple pigments that hide all or part of the yellow. But these pigments appear only if the days are bright and sunny and the nights cool. That is why in some years the leaves are brighter than in others.

While the colors are changing, a thin layer at the base of each leaf stalk becomes hard and dry. It is like a dam that keeps food and water from flowing back and forth between the leaf and the tree. The loosened leaf is no longer a living part of the tree. An autumn shower, a strong wind or even a breeze in the late fall — and the show is over!

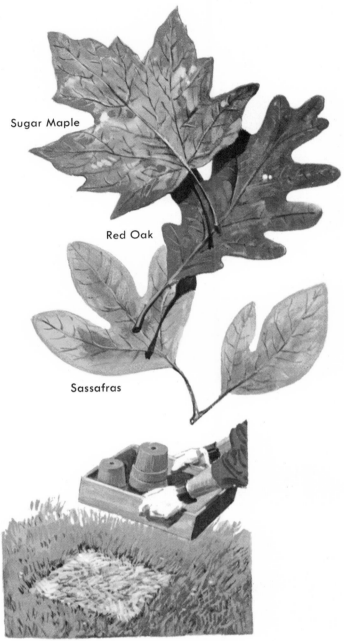

Sugar Maple

Red Oak

Sassafras

Why does grass turn yellow when you cover it up? Perhaps you have gone away and left a box on the lawn for several days. When you pick the box up, you find a yellow square where it covered the grass. But after a few days in sunlight, the grass looks green again. Leaves of grass have the same green pigment that tree leaves have, and they make it for themselves with the help of sunlight. If sunlight is cut off by the box, no green pigment can form. The leaves use up the supply they have on hand; then, when the green is gone, only the yellow pigment is left. If grass goes without sunlight too long, it dies. But if it gets light again in time, it starts making new green pigment.

WHY DO PLANTS WILT?

A BROAD PUMPKIN leaf stands straight and stiff in the early morning. By afternoon it may look droopy, like a hound dog's ears. We say it has wilted. Between sunup and afternoon, the leaf has lost its stiffening material. That material is water!

Of course, water all by itself is not stiff. But think what happens when you fill a hot water bottle as full as you can. It does not droop. A leaf is made of many little sacks of liquid, all joined together. When the sacks are full, the pressure of the water inside holds the leaf firm and straight.

But then the hot sun shines on the plant. Water in the leaves grows warmer. Some of it evaporates through tiny openings. More water may be coming up from the earth, through little tubes in the plant, but it doesn't travel fast enough. The half-empty sacks let the leaf droop.

When the hot sun goes down, the leaves stop losing water. During the night they fill up again. But sometimes it happens that the earth is very dry. The plant roots cannot get enough water from the soil. Then the leaves will stay limp and wilted. After a while, without water, the whole plant dies.

Plants and flowers often wilt when we pick them, then stiffen again after we put them in water. The water goes up through the tubes in their cut stems, just as it does in a growing plant. Sometimes, however, air bubbles get into a cut plant and clog the tubes in the stem. The bubbles keep water out, and so the plant cannot perk up. Gardeners sometimes snip the stems off under water in order to keep air bubbles out.

WHY DOESN'T A HOLLOW TREE DIE?

SOMETIMES a tree gets empty inside, and still it puts out green leaves every spring. The tree doesn't die, because all of the living parts of the trunk are in a narrow band just underneath the bark.

There are many little tubes, only a fraction of an inch thick, in the living part of the tree. Some of these tubes bring water up from the ground into the leaves. Other tubes hold the sap which is a liquid food that the tree's own leaves make for it. The sap also protects the new wood. It acts as an antiseptic and keeps the new wood healthy. As long as there are plenty of tubes all the way up and down a tree trunk, the tree can go on living, even though there may be a big hole inside.

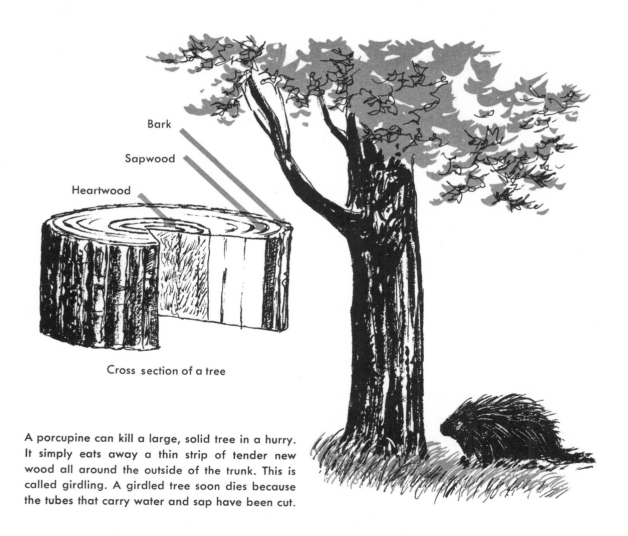

Bark

Sapwood

Heartwood

Cross section of a tree

A porcupine can kill a large, solid tree in a hurry. It simply eats away a thin strip of tender new wood all around the outside of the trunk. This is called girdling. A girdled tree soon dies because the tubes that carry water and sap have been cut.

WHY DO FLOWERS HAVE DIFFERENT COLORS AND SMELLS?

BABY PLANTS grow from seeds, and seeds come from flowers. There are parent plants, just as there are parent animals. When father and mother animals mate, they are likely to walk or swim or fly about, searching for each other until they come together. But flowering plants can't move. Their roots hold them in place. Usually something has to carry a powder called pollen from the male part of one flower to the female part of another flower. The wind carries pollen for some flowers. Insects carry it for others. Birds and even bats do, too.

Most creatures that spread pollen are looking for something to eat. Some insects feed on the pollen itself, but that does no harm because flowers always have plenty to spare. Many flowers hold a sweet juice called nectar that is also good to eat.

An iris is a *bee flower*. Most bee flowers are blue or yellow or a mixture of the two. Very few are red, because a bee's eyes cannot see red.

Butterfly flowers, such as carnations, are often red or orange. Butterflies, unlike bees, can see red.

A magnolia is a *beetle flower.* The beetles seem to pay no attention to color. What attracts them is a strong, sweet odor.

Moth flowers, such as the yellow columbine, are often pale or white. This makes them show up well at dusk or at night when moths visit them.

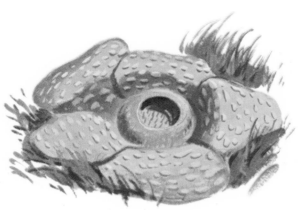

Fly *flowers* are often dull colored. They attract flies mainly by their odor which is somewhat like the smell of spoiled meat.

You can see *wind flowers* if you let your lawn grow long. The flowers of grass plants have no bright colors and no special odor. The wind carries the pollen for them, no matter how they look or how they smell.

The saguaro cactus that grows in Arizona is a *bat flower*. Its white blossoms are open at night when a special kind of bat flies about in search of nectar to eat.

The red columbine is a *bird flower*. Humming birds see red and yellow easily. These are the most usual colors in flowers that birds visit. Birds can't see blue very well.

The pollen carriers locate their food with the help of the flowers themselves. Very often it is color that calls attention to the flower. Or it may be odor. Some blossoms have dark guide lines on a light background, and these lines lead straight to the pollen supply. The shape of the flower may just suit the pollen carrier, too. Some are built exactly right for insects with long tongues. Others fit insects with short tongues. And some are equipped with special landing platforms.

One scientist has divided flowers up according to the way their pollen is carried. Look at the pictures and you will see what some of them are.

Eye

WHY DOES A POTATO HAVE EYES?

THE EYES of a potato are not like your eyes, and they don't see a thing. Just the same, potato eyes are very important, for it is from them that new plants grow each year. The part of the potato that you eat is really a stem, but it grows underground. The eyes are tiny buds. When a stem grows above ground, the buds grow into side branches. The buds on the underground stem of the potato can grow into whole new plants.

At spring planting time, a farmer takes some of last year's potatoes and cuts each one into several pieces, each with an eye in it. He plants these pieces in the earth. Soon each eye sprouts and grows into a new plant. And every new plant forms many new potatoes under the ground.

CAN PLANTS FEEL HURT WHEN THEY ARE CUT?

WHAT HAPPENS when *we* feel a cut? Messages from the cut place travel to the brain. They go along thin white living threads called nerves. Our brains have learned that certain kinds of messages mean "cut" and "hurt."

Plants do not have nerves or brains. We have to say that they can't feel hurt when they are cut.

WHAT MAKES TREES HOLLOW?

THE BARK of a tree helps to protect it from injury, and the wood inside may stay hard and solid for many years. But suppose something injures the bark. Wind or lightning or people break off branches. Insects puncture the bark and lay eggs. Wood-borer grubs, that look like plump worms, make tunnels. Woodpeckers often drill holes to get the grubs. It is easy for certain fungi to enter through openings in the bark. These fungi are relatives of mushrooms, and they feed on wood. Very tiny plants called bacteria also eat wood. The more they eat, the bigger the hole grows, until the entire trunk is hollow.

Men, called tree surgeons, save valuable trees that have developed holes. They scoop out the dead wood, then fill the cavity with cement — in much the same way that a dentist fills a tooth.

HOW CAN PLANTS LIVE UNDER WATER?

PEOPLE cannot live unless they breathe an invisible gas called oxygen which is part of the air. Land plants take a gas from the air, too. It is called carbon dioxide — the same gas that makes soda pop fizz.

Water plants need carbon dioxide. You might think that they get it from air bubbles, but they don't as a rule. The gas is dissolved in the water, just as it is in a bottle of pop. There are gases in streams and lakes and even deep in the ocean. Plants could get carbon dioxide a mile or more below the surface of the sea. But there they cannot get something else they need — sunlight. Light from the sun manages to go only a short way in water before it is stopped. So plants live mainly in shallow water or near the surface of water that is deep.

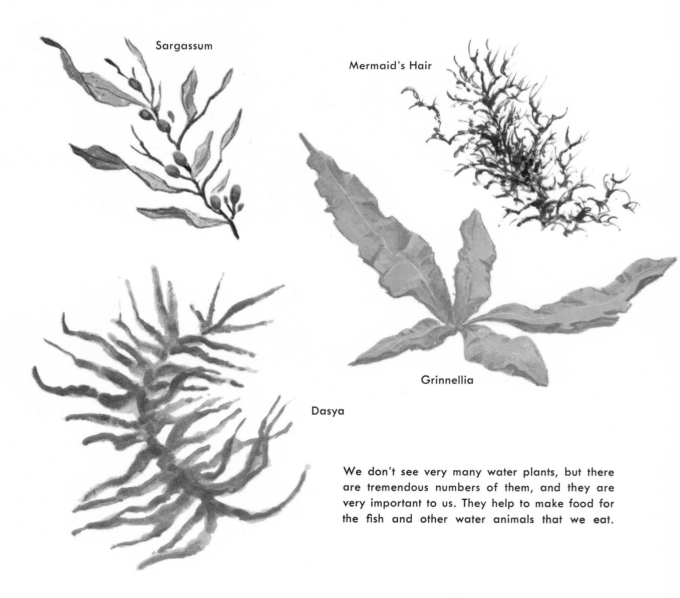

Sargassum

Mermaid's Hair

Grinnellia

Dasya

We don't see very many water plants, but there are tremendous numbers of them, and they are very important to us. They help to make food for the fish and other water animals that we eat.

WHY DO FLOWERS CLOSE UP AT NIGHT?

CALIFORNIA POPPIES fold their petals together when evening comes. So do morning-glories and dandelions and many other flowers. Some of them close up on rainy days, too, and do not open until the sun shines again.

Poppy

The folded petals protect the flower's supply of a yellow powder called pollen. Pollen is important. Unless it is spread from one poppy to another by bees or other insects, the seeds for next year's plants will not form. The insects that visit poppies only fly around on sunny days. If the pollen is kept covered at other times, there will be some on hand when the insects go to work.

Flowers can't figure all this out and fold their petals on purpose. Instead, the petals have a kind of automatic hinge arrangement. Some hinges are kept open by water pressure. Sunlight makes this hinge soak up water from inside the plant. But when the light grows dim, at night or before a storm, the hinge loses water and grows limp. Then the flower closes.

Many flowers don't close up, and they take care of pollen in different ways. The picture shows how a pink lady's-slipper does the trick. A bee lands on top of the blossom near a narrow opening, and in she goes to feast on the juicy hairs inside. The opening is neatly rigged, with curving flaps, so that it can be used only as an entrance. When the bee is ready to leave, she must go out through the exit, straight ahead. It is a tight squeeze. Her back rubs against the ceiling, and that's where the pollen is. The bee sails off with a load of pollen on her back, and delivers it when she rubs against the ceiling of the next lady's-slipper she visits.

WHY DO SOME FLOWERS BLOOM BEFORE OTHERS?

Violets bloom in the spring. Chrysanthemums bloom in the fall. Flowers of the ragweed plant begin to open up in summer, on an exact date, year after year. Many other plants behave as if they, too, had built-in alarm clocks, all set to go off at special times.

Some of the flower clocks are set to go off when nights are short and days are long. The ragweed, for instance, blooms when the day is divided into ten hours of darkness and fourteen hours of daylight. Other flowers need more than ten hours of darkness. That is why chrysanthemums bloom in the fall, when days are short and nights are long.

Scientists did experiments to learn these secrets of the flower clocks, and they soon discovered that they could set the clocks forward or back! A chrysanthemum would bloom ahead of time if it was kept in a dark place from late afternoon until late morning. The man-made night was as good as a naturally long night. On the other hand, the flowers would *not* bloom if a light was turned on near them for a few minutes after dark. The light made two short nights out of a long one.

These experiments were useful to flower growers. If you look into a greenhouse in September, you may see plants covered with a black cloth. This black tent is a "long-night maker." It will speed up the clocks, so that florists will have blossoms to sell ahead of the regular flowering time.

Experiments with light and darkness gave scientists only part of the information they were looking for. They did not find out what made a plant act as if it could tell time by its own clock. They saw it happen, but they were not sure how it was done.

Scientists do know about a special plant chemical that seems to act like a switch going on and off. Light and darkness change the switch back and forth. Every kind of green plant has some of this switching material, but each one uses it in a different way at different times, and so the flower clocks run on their own particular schedules.

Buttercup

Morning Glory

Sunflower

Thistle

WHAT IS A WEED?

IF YOU ASK a scientist what a weed is, he will say it is any plant that grows where man does not want it to grow. So a rose in a field of cabbages is a weed! Most people are always pulling dandelions out of their lawns. But farmers who grow dandelions for salad greens pull grass out instead.

There are some plants that nobody wants for any purpose. These weeds keep growing even though gardeners, year after year, do their best to get rid of them. Some, like quack grass, multiply from underground stems. Every time you chop a stem into pieces with a hoe, you are actually making more new quack grass plants.

Many weeds produce enormous numbers of seeds every year. Scientists counted the seeds from a single plant of hedge mustard one year and found that there were 511,000. Some weeds, such as burdocks and beggar-ticks, have seeds that stick to your clothes, and so they hitchhike to new locations. The seeds of milkweed have tiny silky parachutes attached to them. They can float long distances on the slightest breeze.

Sometimes plants start out as garden plants, then spread by themselves so wildly that they become weeds. Bachelor's-button, Star-of-Bethlehem and chicory annoy farmers and gardeners. But we can still enjoy the beauty they add to roadsides and open fields.

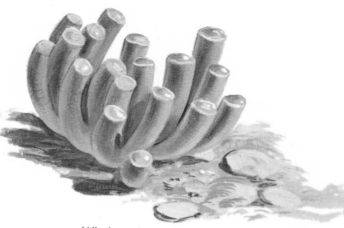

Some plants that grow in the African desert have built-in windows! The plants live almost completely buried in the earth. Only the tops stick out, and they are covered with a glassy looking skin that lets in sunlight but keeps moisture from escaping. The flowers burst out of the windows when they bloom.

Window plant — *Fenestraria Aurantiaca*

Hedgehog Cactus

Organ Pipe Cactus

HOW CAN CACTUS PLANTS LIVE IN THE DESERT?

MOST PLANTS have leaves that allow drops of moisture to escape into the air. But not the cactus. It has very few leaves, sometimes none. The prickly pear cactus looks as if it has enormous leaves, but these are only broad, flat joints in its stem.

A cactus has roots that grow near the surface of the earth, and they can pick up rain or even heavy dew before the moisture evaporates. Since the inside parts of the plant are like sponges, they can soak up a great deal of water and store it to use in dry weather. Wherever you see a cactus, you can be sure it gets moisture sometimes, no matter how waterless the desert around it seems to be.

108

WHAT IS THE DIFFERENCE BETWEEN MUSHROOMS AND TOADSTOOLS?

LONG AGO people believed that toads used certain mushrooms as stools to sit on. People also believed that toads were poisonous. So it was easy to go on and say that *toad stools* were poisonous mushrooms.

The trouble is that toads aren't deadly poisonous, and few, if any, of them ever sit on mushrooms. Besides, there is no easy way to tell which mushrooms are poisonous and which are not. Altogether the word toadstool is not a very good one to use. Stick to *mushroom*.

Scientists have found about seventy different kinds of mushrooms that can kill people or make them very sick. They also know that about seven hundred kinds are entirely safe to eat. But it often takes a real expert to tell a mushroom that is delicious from one that is deadly. The only safe rule to follow is this: *Never eat wild mushrooms*. Go to the store instead and get the kind that have been carefully grown for food.

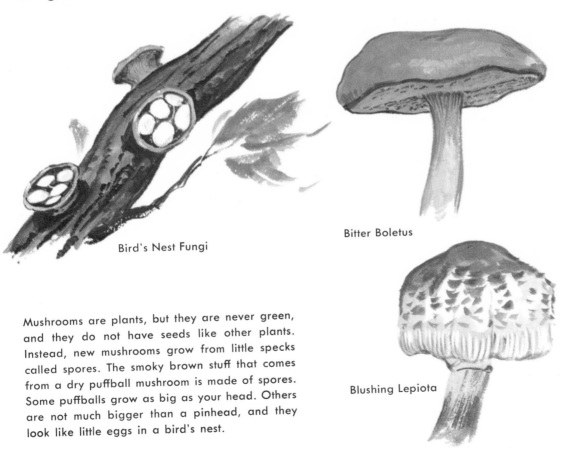

Bird's Nest Fungi

Bitter Boletus

Blushing Lepiota

Mushrooms are plants, but they are never green, and they do not have seeds like other plants. Instead, new mushrooms grow from little specks called spores. The smoky brown stuff that comes from a dry puffball mushroom is made of spores. Some puffballs grow as big as your head. Others are not much bigger than a pinhead, and they look like little eggs in a bird's nest.

WHY DO PEOPLE SNORE?

YOU CAN SNORE when you are awake. Just let all the stiffness go out of the soft flap at the back and top of your mouth. Then you take a strong, deep breath with your mouth open. The flap moves back and forth, like a window shade fluttering in the wind, and the noise it makes is a snore.

When you sleep, your mouth and throat relax, and often you breathe deeply. The fluttering in your throat increases if you sleep on your back. It usually stops if you turn on your side — or if you make so much noise that you wake yourself up.

Men usually snore more than women. Nobody knows exactly why.

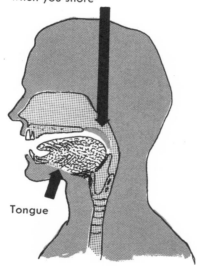

This part of mouth vibrates when you snore

Tongue

HOW CAN WE SMELL THINGS?

THE AIR is a mixture of many different tiny particles. Most of them are so small that you cannot see or feel them. When you breathe, some of these particles dissolve in the liquid which keeps the inside of your nose moist. And then something may happen. Suddenly you say "Cinnamon!" or "Roses!" or "Skunk!" You have smelled an odor.

The inside of your nose is a kind of chemical laboratory for smelling. It can detect unbelievably small amounts of odor. This is how it works:

The odor particles dissolve in liquid. Together, the particles and the liquid form a chemical which touches the ends of very small nerves in the nose. A message goes along these nerves to the brain, and there the odor is recognized, *if* you have smelled it before. If you have not smelled it before, your brain makes a record of the new odor and you will remember it next time you smell it. Most people can remember tens of thousands of different smells.

If your nose is absolutely dry, you cannot smell anything. And things have no odor if they cannot be dissolved in the liquid in the nose. This is true of all creatures. Many fish have a very good sense of smell, and of course they do all their smelling in water, not in air.

Long ago, the first living creatures were water animals, and many of them could smell, but not see or hear. The brains of these animals had more to do with smell than with anything else. Odor led them to food and warned them about enemies. Scientists call these brains *nose-brains*. The parts of our brains that are now connected with seeing and hearing and thinking all come from the nose-brain of those early creatures who were our ancient ancestors. So a nose is very important, even though you don't use it the way other animals do.

Blending perfume

Gathering roses for perfume

WHY CAN'T YOU DRINK SALT WATER WHEN YOU ARE SHIPWRECKED?

"WATER, WATER, everywhere, nor any drop to drink," said the sailor in a famous poem. This was his way of explaining that you can be terribly thirsty out in the ocean, even with water all around you.

Everyone needs both salt and water. But the amount of salt in the body must be kept exactly right, and that is the job of two bean-shaped parts of the body called kidneys. If there is too much salt, the kidneys wash it away with water. Have you ever noticed that when you eat salty fish you feel thirsty? You need extra water to wash out the extra salt that your body cannot use.

Ocean water has a great deal of salt. A drink of ocean water soon makes you thirsty, and the kidneys need to wash the extra salt away. But if you take another drink of sea water to wash away the salt from the first drink, you only put more salt into your body, and you need still *more* fresh water to wash it out. You may feel better for a while after drinking ocean water, but soon the extra salt in your body makes you sick.

Some birds have to drink salt water because they never leave the sea. They have special parts called glands, just above the eyes, which get rid of the salt in a liquid like tears. One kind of bird squirts the salty water out through tubes like water guns above its beak.

WHY DO YOU HAVE TO SLEEP?

As a rule, girls and boys have to go to sleep because someone says it is time for bed. But if you stay up long past bedtime, you discover that you would rather go to sleep than do anything else in the world.

People have made experiments with staying awake for long periods of time. After two days they got very cross, and they didn't think very well. Your brain is like a shop where waste materials pile up because of all the work that goes on. At night while you are asleep the work slows down, and there is a chance for cleaners to carry the wastes away.

Shark

A bear's winter sleep is called hibernation.

The older you are, the less sleep you seem to need. But even the oldest person needs several hours a day. Animals are different. A rat sleeps about half the time. An elephant gets along with a two or three hour nap. Elephants and horses can sleep standing up. Sharks hardly seem to sleep at all. They just doze for a few minutes now and then. Bears sleep all winter.

WHEN YOU GO to sleep, the part of you that pays attention to the outside world takes a rest. Usually your eyes close, so that your brain does not get signals about things that you can see. Although a very loud noise may disturb you, ordinary sounds do not reach the part of you that usually listens. You stop thinking and planning, and you lose the sense of being yourself which is called consciousness.

At the same time, your body goes right on doing some things automatically. You breathe. Your heart beats. The little separate parts of your body called cells use food and oxygen. Some of the cells that have worn out during the day are replaced. And, if your body is still not grown-up, you get a little bigger while you sleep.

What are dreams? Sleeping or waking, you have thoughts and feelings which cause tiny electric signals in your brain. When you are asleep, the thoughts and feelings are dreams. Scientists don't know why we have dreams, but they have invented a way of studying them. First, they ask someone to go to sleep with wires held by tape to his face, near the eyes. The wires record the movements his eyes make. Every once in a while he is awakened so that he can tell about his dreams. Then the scientists can check the dreams with the eye movements. They have found that during a dream your eyes dart back and forth, exactly as if you were watching a show on a stage! A dream seems to be your own private show.

WHY DO YOU SHIVER WHEN YOU ARE COLD?

SHIVERING WARMS you up. When you shiver and shake, your muscles are doing work. They are exercising. Work and exercise make you warm.

A shiver is a special kind of exercise. You do it without thinking. At the same time, something else happens in your body. Suddenly there is a shut-down in the little tubes that carry warm blood just underneath your skin. The blood stays deeper down in your body, where it helps to warm your heart and liver and other important organs. Although your skin feels chilly when you shiver, you are warming yourself inside.

What makes you start to shiver? What makes you stop? Is there an automatic switch in your body that turns the shivers on and off? Experiments have proved that there is a spot on the under side of the brain which does work like a switch.

Another switch, in this same part of the brain, keeps your body from getting too hot. If the heat goes up, this switch turns on a signal. More blood goes to the skin, and you begin to sweat more. Sweat carries away heat, and your body is cooled. Then the switch turns off and sweating slows down.

The switches act like a sort of thermostat, and so your temperature stays about the same as long as you are well. When you are sick, the thermostat may get upset, and then you have a fever.

Doctors still don't know exactly what upsets the thermostat, but they do have an idea that may turn out to be right. They believe that diseases cause changes in the little bits of material called white cells in the blood. These white cells now give off a special chemical. The chemical affects the thermostat in your brain — and up goes your temperature.

Porpoise

Cobra

Pelican

Frog

Flying Fish

Big Horn

People belong to a large group of animals that are called *warm-blooded*. So do cats, dogs, and all other creatures that feed their babies with their own milk. Birds are warm-blooded, too. Snakes, frogs, fish, and lizards are all called *cold-blooded*. They do not have automatic switches and thermostats that keep their bodies evenly warmed. Instead, the cold-blooded animal is warm when the world around it is warm. It is cold when its surroundings are chilly.

115

WHY DO TEETH GET LOOSE?

WHEN YOU WERE born, your first teeth were already starting to grow, but nobody could see them. They still had to poke their way through your gums. It took two or three years for all of them to appear.

First teeth are always small, because they have to fit into small jaws. As a baby grows, the jawbones grow, too. But the first teeth stay the same size. Meanwhile, more teeth and bigger ones are growing and pushing upward inside the gums. The first teeth get loose and usually they drop out all by themselves.

Dog's teeth

Beaver

The tusks of a wild boar are really teeth that have grown so long that they stick out of his mouth. An elephant's tusks are extra-large teeth, too.

A deer has front teeth only in the lower jaw. When it snips off leaves to eat, it presses the teeth against a soft pad in the upper jaw.

All the furry animals have two sets of teeth, just as people do. You can tell interesting things about what an animal eats by looking at the kind of teeth it has. A dog has two long ones at each side of its mouth. These are called *canines*, which means *dog*, and they are useful for tearing meat. Animals such as the rabbit have front teeth that keep on growing all through life, but are worn down by constant nibbling on hard food. Cows have large, flat grinding teeth for chewing coarse grass. People eat both vegetables and meat, and they have cutting teeth at the front and grinding teeth at the back.

WHY DO YOU GET GOOSE PIMPLES?

WHEN YOU ARE frightened or cold, little bumps sometimes form on your skin. These are called goose pimples or goose flesh. At the center of each bump is a hair in a tiny tube. And near the tubes are small muscles that can tighten and pull, so that the hairs stand up straighter than usual.

If something scares you suddenly, a special little pouch in your body squirts a chemical out into your blood. This chemical makes certain muscles tighten up, including muscles in your skin. The picture shows how a tight muscle makes a goose pimple. Your hair really does stand on end when you are scared.

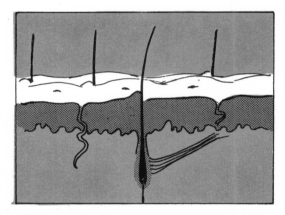

A sudden chill can make these same skin muscles pull tight. The bumps disappear when you feel warm again.

If you have ever seen a goose before it was cooked, you know how the bumps got their name. Real goose flesh is covered with bumps where the feathers grow.

Anger or fear can fluff up the hair of cats and other animals. Perhaps this may help to frighten off enemies. It may also fool a biting enemy, so that his teeth sink into fur instead of flesh. Cold weather, too, causes tight muscles in animals' skins. Their fur stands up, and motionless air fills the spaces between hairs. Since heat does not pass easily through still air, the animal's body keeps warm. That is why your cat can stay outdoors in freezing weather. Birds can, too. They fluff out their feathers.

What causes hiccups? Sometimes the messages that take care of breathing get mixed up with other messages. For instance, a very cold drink may irritate your stomach, which is close to a big sheet of muscle that helps to work the pumping of your lungs. Suddenly, when the muscle gets ready to let in air, a mix-up happens. A wrong signal goes to a certain little flap in your throat. The flap closes off your windpipe. Now no air can go into your lungs. Because of the wrong signals, two sets of muscles are working against each other. The big sheet of muscle gives a jerk. The smack of the closing flap, plus the jerk, makes a hiccup.

WHY DO YOU YAWN?

WHEN YOU YAWN, it almost always means that you are tired. A tired body slows down. It does not get rid of all the waste materials that form in muscles and other parts of you. One of these wastes is a gas called carbon dioxide or CO_2. Too much CO_2 in your body makes you yawn. You open your mouth wide, take in an enormous breath of air, and then push out a big breath that carries CO_2 away.

All of this goes on automatically, because a special part of your brain acts like a switchboard sending out messages that take care of breathing as a rule. An extra lot of CO_2 in the brain seems to flip an emergency switch, and messages go to all the muscles that are used when you yawn.

Sometimes you yawn just after someone else does. That is because the messages can be started by other things besides CO_2. Sights and sounds affect your breathing. The sight of somebody else's yawn is enough to make your own muscles start to work automatically. You may be yawning now, just from reading this!

IS RADIATION DANGEROUS?

RADIATION IS a word that scientists used when they discovered something mysterious and invisible that took photographs in the dark. They found it shooting out of certain rocks and chemicals. They found it in a special kind of electric light bulb. Sometimes it behaved like light or like particles of electricity, and sometimes like fast-moving bits of actual material.

We know more about radiation now. One kind has turned out to be electrical particles. Another kind is material, and another can be called little bundles of energy. All of them are very powerful, and they can enter the body like invisible bullets. A large number of these radiation bullets coming all at once can destroy living material. Even a small number may do strange things to ordinary chemicals that make up the body. By changing one chemical into another, radiation can do damage. Some kinds of radiation can keep the body from rebuilding worn-out parts.

But radiation may also help people who are sick. A skillful doctor can use it to take pictures and discover broken bones. He can aim the invisible bullets at a particular spot and destroy something that is harming the body.

Scientists still do not know all of the good things or all of the bad things about radiation, and so they must take very great care not to let it do more harm than good.

HOW DO WE SEE?

WE GET information about the world in many ways. Seeing is one of them. Our eyes tell us about shape, color, size, and distance. They tell us who is who. They give us knowledge and countless pleasures. To do this, they have millions of tiny parts that work with light and electricity.

The front of the eye is somewhat like a camera: It has a lens that collects rays of light. Just as a camera has film, the back of the eye has a special layer that changes when light strikes it. Light bleaches the material in the eye film and makes ever-changing pictures there.

The living film in the eye is made of many bits of material called cells. Some of the cells are shaped like rods. An eye has about 100 million of these! Other cells look like sharpened pencils. They are called cones, and an eye has about 6 million of them. The cones allow us to see color. The rods show everything in black, white and gray.

All of these millions of cells have a sort of electrical connection to the inner part of the brain. When a pattern of light flashes onto the film of rods and cones, millions of electric signals make a pattern inside the brain, and we see.

Hawk

Hawk in flight

Why can a hawk see better than we can? We see the separate letters on this page because each dark letter is surrounded by a white area. Light reflected from the white paper strikes some of those millions of electric connections in our eyes and makes a clear pattern. In one particularly important spot, a hawk's eyes have three times as many connections as ours do, and so the pattern of things seen is clearer. If we had a hawk's eyes, we could look out of the top window of a skyscraper and see a dime on the sidewalk.

120

HOW DO WE TASTE THINGS?

TASTING begins in the tongue. Its tip and edges and back part are dotted with little bumps that have holes in them. Beneath the holes lie small knobs that look like flower buds. They are called taste buds, and long threads called nerves connect each one to your brain. The buds on different parts of the tongue are good at tasting different things.

Suppose you put a drop of syrup on the *tip* of your tongue. The syrup drips through the holes onto the buds. Signals go quickly along the threads to your brain, and you say to yourself, "Sweet!" If you put a drop of sweet syrup on the back of your tongue, you won't taste it, because the buds at the very back detect only bitter things. A drop of vinegar on either side of the tongue, will make you say, "Sour!" The buds that detect salty things are on the front and sides. Sweet, bitter, salt and sour are the four different tastes that everybody agrees on. Some people add soapy and metallic tastes to the list. No matter what you put in your mouth, its taste is one of these — or a combination of several.

The *flavor* of food is something else. It can be a combination of tastes, plus an odor that is detected by your nose. The smell and taste of food are closely linked. You find this out when you have a cold. If your nose is very stuffy, you cannot taste the difference between a piece of apple and a piece of onion!

You cannot taste a lump of sugar, either, if you wipe your tongue very dry before putting the sugar in your mouth. Things can be tasted only when they are dissolved in a liquid, such as the saliva in your mouth.

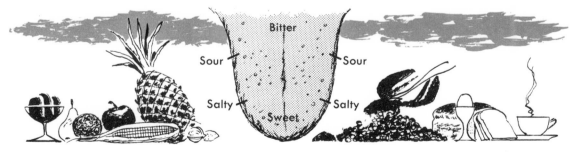

Things often taste different to different people. There is a special chemical which almost everybody calls bitter. But a few people cannot taste it at all. Another chemical is sweet or bitter to three out of four people, but one out of four finds it tasteless. These differences seem to come to you from your parents, just as the color of your eyes does, but, so far, nobody knows why this is so.

HOW DO YOU GROW?

DO YOU REMEMBER the time when you could walk under the kitchen table without hitting your head? Then one day you tried it, and — *bump!* The table legs hadn't grown shorter, but something had been added to your legs. In fact, something had been added to your whole body.

Your body is made of materials arranged in small bundles called cells. There are bone cells and muscle cells and skin cells and many others. Each cell is a hard-working part of you. Each one takes in food and then changes that food into two new cells exactly like itself. This remarkable work goes on day and night.

Most cells are so small that you can see them only with a microscope. But there are many millions of them. One million bone cells split into two million. Then two million split and make four million. No wonder your legs get longer! Skin cells divide and cover up your longer legs. Dividing cells also make longer muscles and longer tubes to carry blood.

All this seems like a very well-run building job, with bricklayers, plumbers, and plasterers carrying out a plan on schedule. All building projects have a boss and helpers who take messages around, and your body also has helpers. Its messengers are chemicals. They come from special parts called glands. One very important gland in your body sends out a great many very powerful chemicals. Some of these go straight to the cells themselves. Some direct other glands that in turn keep the cells working and growing. These things go on according to a built-in pattern.

You get taller because the messages make the cells in your legs and spine grow. But when you are about twenty years old a change takes place. The glands send out new signals that mean the bones are long enough. Your built-in plan for growing up is completed. From now on, the glands and the chemical messengers are more like handymen who keep things in running order and repair worn-out parts.

WHY DO YOU BLINK YOUR EYES?

You BLINK your eyes to protect them from a sudden bright light and to keep them clean. The moving lids push tears over the eyeballs and the tears wash away any dust particles. The tears do another thing, too. They make it easy for the lids to slide up and down.

A small pouch called a gland, above your eyes, keeps on making tears all the time. An oily substance on the rims of your lids keeps the tears from spilling over and running down your face. Instead, they collect in the corner of your eye and then go through a tube into your nose.

When you are hurt or frightened, a gland inside your body squirts out a chemical that makes the tear glands work extra hard. Your eyes suddenly fill up with tears. There are so many that they may spill over, in spite of the oily rims of your eyelids.

Even when you are crying hard and your eyes are full of tears, you keep on blinking your eyelids. Now they are clearing away tears, not dust. They are acting like windshield wipers in the rain.

WHY DO WE HAVE "CRAZY BONES"?

THE "CRAZY BONE"—or "funny bone"—is not a bone at all. It is a place near your elbow where little bundles of nerves run along under the skin without much protection. These nerves, which look like white threads, carry messages from your hand and lower arm, across the elbow, and on to your brain. If you touch a hot dish or a piece of ice, if you cut your finger, squash your thumb, scratch your wrist, itch, ache, tingle, or feel anything else, nerves carry the information up your arm and to your brain.

Usually a message starts at the tip end of a nerve. But it *can* start somewhere else along the line.

Now suppose you get a sharp whack on the spot where bundles of nerves stretch across the hard, bony elbow joint. Two things happen: nerves in the elbow itself signal "Hurt!" And other nerves — the ones which usually carry messages from their tip ends in the hand and lower arm—also begin to carry pain messages all at the same time. The result is like a whole pack of firecrackers exploding at once. Crazy is a good word for the mixup that you feel.

The pitcher sent a ball high to the inside, and this left-handed batter caught it on the "crazy bone."

WHY IS BLOOD RED?

IF YOU LOOK at a drop of blood from a cut finger, all you can see is solid red color. But if you look at blood through a microscope, you will see separate red bits floating about like round rafts. These rafts are called cells, and the red color is a chemical inside them. Its name is hemoglobin.

The red blood cells travel constantly, because blood itself travels through tubes all over the body, carrying food and other necessary things. One of these things is oxygen, which comes from the air that you breathe into your lungs. Oxygen helps your body to use the food that you have eaten. Between meals the body can store up food and use it slowly. But it cannot store up enough oxygen. A fresh supply must keep coming in. It must be picked up and carried to every part of the body. The red blood cells do the pick-up job. As they pass through tubes in the lungs, bits of oxygen push into the tubes and join the red hemoglobin. On they go until the red cells reach a place where body cells need the oxygen. The hemoglobin parts from the oxygen, but it keeps on traveling inside its cell rafts. It picks up more oxygen when it gets back to the lungs.

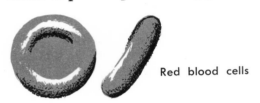

Red blood cells

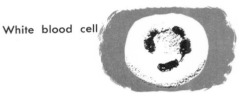

White blood cell

WHY ARE SOME PEOPLE LEFT-HANDED?

VERY YOUNG babies sometimes begin to use one hand more than the other. By the time girls and boys go to school, they are almost always either right-handed or left-handed. When we ask why, we are likely to get several different answers. Some people think that a small child may begin to use one hand more than the other just by chance, and the habit stays with him. Or, if he has a left-handed parent, he may be imitating. Or he may be born with a kind of pattern that makes him use his left hand, while other people have a right-handed pattern.

So far as anyone knows, left-handed and right-handed people can learn how to do exactly the same things. In countries like ours, a "leftie" finds writing a little hard, because he has to work from left to right, and he can't see what he has just written. In some countries, writing goes from right to left, and there a right-handed person has trouble!

A few people can use both hands equally well. We say they are ambidextrous. Doctors think that this kind of skill can't be learned. You are either born with it or you are not.

WHEN YOU SNEEZE, a strong blast of air blows away something that is irritating your nose. You don't decide whether or not to sneeze. The blast of air just comes automatically.

Suppose you have breathed in some pepper. A message goes to your brain from the peppered spot in your nose. Immediately your brain sends another message to the muscles that make your lungs work like an air pump. The air-pumping muscles give a sudden hard squeeze. Out comes a gust of breath, as fast as a hurricane wind. It may be going 200 miles an hour! The pepper is blown away.

Various things can irritate the tender lining of your nose. Pollen from grass or flowers bothers some people. We say they are allergic to these pollens, or that they have hay fever. And, of course, a cold can make you sneeze.

Once you start to sneeze, it is almost impossible to stop just by making up your mind to do so. You can block a sneeze, though, if you press hard on your upper lip. Press until it hurts a little. When you do this, your nerves carry pain signals, and your brain pays more attention to them than to the irritation signals from your nose. As a result, your brain doesn't finish sending the message that tells the muscles around your lungs to make you sneeze.

Russian Wolfhound

English Setter

Dachshund

Did you ever watch a dog sneeze? He keeps his mouth shut. When you sneeze, you usually open yours. A dog has nearly a straight line from his nose into his lungs. Nothing gets in the way of the air that his lungs push out. But people have developed such big brains that their noses have been shoved out of line.

WHEN you run, your muscles work very hard. In order to work, they must have food and oxygen. Of course, you don't have to eat while you run. Your body stores up food between meals. But you do have to keep breathing and getting oxygen from the air. If you run fast, you breathe deeply. The extra oxygen that you take in may not be quite enough for your hard-working muscles, but they can borrow a little from various parts of the body. Then when you stop running, the oxygen has to be paid back. You keep on panting and taking in extra air until the borrowed oxygen has been returned.

WHAT MAKES YOUR FOOT GO TO SLEEP?

WHEN YOUR FOOT feels prickly, you say it has gone to sleep. This often happens after you have been sitting with your leg doubled up. A doubled-up leg is like a water hose with a kink in it. Just as the water only trickles through the hose, the blood runs slowly through the blood vessels. It cannot go fast enough to do its regular jobs. One of these jobs is picking up garbage—carrying away the body's wastes and leftovers. When the wastes can't be taken away as usual, they interfere with the work of fine threads called nerves which carry messages from your foot to your brain. Your brain can't tell what is happening in your foot.

Now suppose you stand up. There is no more pressure to slow down the blood and stop the nerve messages. Suddenly a whole group of messages begin pouring into your brain. The nerves have actually been a little bit poisoned by the waste materials that piled up. This gives you a feeling that pins and needles are sticking into your foot. The prickling disappears when the blood flows regularly again and the nerves have nothing to make them excited.

HOW DO WE HEAR?

THE OUTSIDE part of the ear acts like a funnel to catch invisible sound waves in the air. These waves are started by a beating drum or a barking dog or anything else that makes a sound. Another name for a sound wave is vibration.

After the vibrations in the air are funneled into your head, a whole chain of things begins to happen. Stretched across the end of the funnel is a thin skin like the head of a drum. Sound waves make it vibrate. The vibrating eardrum moves a bone that touches it. This bone moves another bone which moves another. The last bone sets up waves in a liquid, and

these waves make thousands of tiny hairs wiggle back and forth. The vibrating hairs are connected in a very complicated way with your brain. Your brain can tell one kind of vibration from another, and you hear noises or words or music or other sounds.

You can train yourself to shut out some sounds while you listen to others. An orchestra leader can listen to each separate instrument, even though many instruments are playing together. And he can tell which player is making a mistake!

"YOU ARE ALLERGIC to poison ivy," the doctor says. He means that your skin gets watery, itchy spots after you touch a poison-ivy plant. This is what happens:

There is a special chemical in poison ivy. You have a different special chemical in your body. When the two join together, a third chemical wakes up, as if it were answering a knock at the door. This third one is called histamine, and ordinarily it does no harm. But when it is called out like this, it becomes very active. It makes liquid collect under your skin. It makes small blood vessels get larger, so that the skin is swollen wherever the histamine goes to work.

Some people are allergic to the special chemicals in dust, or smoke, or a powder called pollen that comes from flowers. Histamine makes these people sneeze or wheeze. Foods can cause allergies, too. They can make people itch or have stomach-aches. Doctors still don't know why some of us have allergies while others do not. They do know how to use medicines that help overcome allergies. One kind of medicine, called anti-histamine, often keeps the histamine from running wild.

Sumac

Poison Ivy

WHAT MAKES US BLUSH?

THE WAY WE feel about things can have an effect on the way our bodies work. When we feel embarrassed or upset, tiny blood vessels under the skin grow larger. More blood flows close to the surface. The skin has more color than usual, and it feels very warm because the extra blood brings extra heat along. This is a blush. We do not know exactly how or why it happens. As a rule, we can't stop a blush by thinking about it, but it goes away by itself in a few moments.

Some people turn very pale when they get upset. This is because the blood vessels have tightened up, so that less blood shows through the skin.

HOW DOES YOUR BODY BURN UP THE FOOD YOU EAT?

FOOD IS FUEL, and fuel burns. But where is the fire?

The fact is that burning can be either fast or slow. A log in a fire burns very fast. As it burns, the different chemical combinations in the wood shuffle around. Some of the chemicals join with oxygen from the air. In a little while the whole log has changed and disappeared, except for a few ashes.

Some of the wood chemicals are also in food. They, too, change and join with the oxygen that you breathe into your body. But the shuffling goes on a little at a time. It warms you without making you glow like a fire.

HOW MANY HAIRS DOES A PERSON HAVE ON HIS HEAD?

BALD PEOPLE have only a few hairs. Some people have as many as half a million. Most of us have about 120,000 hairs on our heads.

How did anyone ever count that many? If you could count 50 hairs a minute, every minute, ten hours a day, it would take you four full days to finish one ordinary head. There is an easier way to do this kind of job. First you mark off a square patch of scalp, one inch on every side, and count only the hairs in this patch. Suppose there are a thousand. Then you measure the scalp and find out how big it is — how many one-inch patches there are on it. Suppose there are 150 patches. This means there would be one thousand times 150 hairs on the whole head.

WHY DO WE HAVE TO GO TO SCHOOL?

BIRDS and beetles and bears — most animals in the world — are born with a great deal of ready-made knowledge. When a bird or a beetle is old enough to fly, it doesn't need to be taught how. Even if a bear went to school for a very long time, it couldn't learn much more than a few tricks. But without any teaching it will climb trees and hunt for a place to curl up when cold weather comes.

You are different. When you were born, your brain was much bigger than a baby animal's brain, but you had much less ready-made knowledge. You couldn't swim like a baby fish or get up and walk and scratch around for your dinner like a newly-hatched chick. You had to learn the simplest things. School began for you the first time you ever used your eyes to see and your ears to hear and your fingers and toes to feel.

Children everywhere go to schools of some kind, even when they don't learn reading and writing. An Eskimo father is a teacher, and his son learns how to hunt for seals. An Indian mother teaches her daughter how to cook and weave baskets. Your school saves you a great deal of time and trouble, because you learn in a few years what it took men and women thousands of years to find out. Besides, the things you find out make life much more interesting than if you were a bird or a beetle or a bear.

PEOPLE began measuring the days and nights a long, long while ago. Suppose a man took his sheep every morning to a good pasture far from home. Of course he wanted to know when to start back for dinner, and he found that he could tell by watching the shadows move across the earth as the sun moved across the sky. Then someone noticed that the stars, too, moved in regular ways in the night sky. Men could measure time by the positions of shadows and of stars.

In a country called Babylonia, ideas about time became part of people's religion, because the priests studied the sun and the stars. They decided to divide the day and the night into 12 parts each, or 24 altogether. The priests in Egypt had this idea, too, and they invented 12 gods of the night hours who were supposed to pull the Sun God's boat through a dark underground tunnel so that the sun could come up again in the morning.

Sundial

Hourglass

Before clocks were invented people told time by sundials which measured shadows. They also kept track of the hours with a sand glass or hourglass. The sand in the top part of the glass took just a half-hour to run down into the bottom part. Then it had to be turned over.

Stop watch

Roman chariot

The custom of having a twelve-hour day and a twelve-hour night went from one country to another. But the hours weren't always the same length. In summer, each of the 12 daytime hours was longer than each of the 12 nighttime hours, because daylight lasts longer than darkness in summer. In Egypt or Rome, a summer daylight hour could have 80 minutes while a night hour would be only 40 minutes long. When winter came, night had the long hours and day had the short ones.

The Romans were very strict about time. They made a rule that people could only drive a chariot around the city during the last two hours of their twelve-hour day. This meant that in summer they could take long rides before sundown. But in winter only short rides were possible.

These changeable hours worked all right for ancient people. But they were no good at all when men began to build machines and do scientific experiments that needed accurate timing. And imagine trying to bake a cake for exactly 1 hour if you lived in ancient Rome.

SUPPOSE a baby is born on February 29, 1960. The next three Februarys have only 28 days. There is not another February 29 until the year 1964. What about the baby's birthdays? How can he have one every year? Will he be only five years old when other boys born in 1960 are twenty years old?

Of course he will be just as old as the others. And he can choose his own birthday — either February 28 or March 1. The years that have the extra days are called *leap years*. Once there was a law about people born on February 29 in England. The law said that these people had a right to call February 28 their birthday, except in leap years.

ARE PEOPLE REALLY NINE FEET TALL IN AFRICA?

No. But the tallest people in the world do live in Africa. In the Watusi tribe most of the men are seven feet tall, and a few are a little taller. Watusi women are nearly seven feet.

A PYGMY is a member of a tribe of small people who live in certain forests in Africa. A perfectly normal grown-up Pygmy man may be four and a half feet tall, or sometimes a little more.

A midget is a small person who never grows to be as big as his parents or the other normal people he lives among. He stays small because something happens to certain parts of his body called glands. If these glands do not work properly, the body stops growing. There are midgets among many different kinds of people. There might even be midget Pygmies!

About a hundred years ago a famous midget belonged to the circus. His nickname was Tom Thumb. This is how he looked standing beside a large dictionary.

CAN ANYBODY LIVE IN THE SAHARA DESERT?

PEOPLE do live in the Sahara Desert. They have discovered springs or dug wells here and there. A place that has enough water for a camping place or a village is called an oasis.

Some wandering shepherd people move their sheep and goats from one oasis to another. Fierce warriors called Tuaregs also are desert dwellers. Tuareg men wear blue veils that protect their faces from the sun.

THIS YEAR there are more people in the world than last year. Next year there will be still more. And so on. But you don't need to worry. There is room enough for a great many more. We have plenty of material for building homes to live in and cities to work in. Most important, we can grow enough food for everybody.

The huge deserts in North and South America, in Africa and Asia and Australia will make wonderful farmlands as soon as they can get water. And scientists already know how to solve the problem. They can take the salt out of sea water. This way of getting fresh water is still expensive, but inventors are working on better machines to do the job. When these are built, they can pump fresh water to any dry spot in the world.

You have probably heard that in some parts of the world people do not get enough to eat. That is true. If millions of people are hungry now, won't there be still more hungry people when the world gets more crowded?

The answer is this: There could be enough to feed everybody if farmers everywhere used good modern machines and modern ways of growing food. The farms in the United States could grow three times as much food as they do now, and they already grow so much that a great deal is wasted or thrown away. What we need to do is make better plans, so that everybody gets the food that farms can grow. This shouldn't be too hard for human beings who have already invented ways of turning sea water into fresh water that will change deserts into gardens.

Irrigating an orange grove

Pump

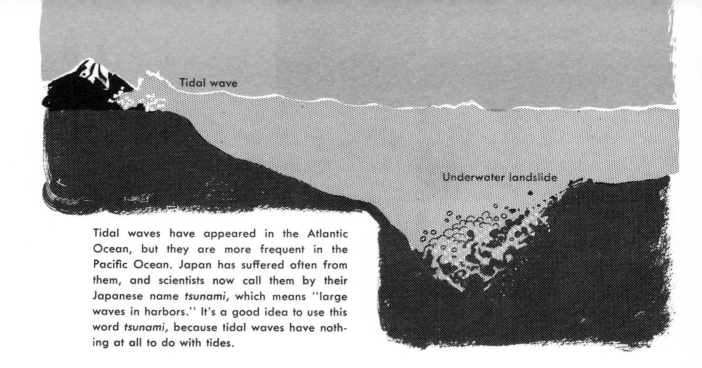

Tidal wave

Underwater landslide

Tidal waves have appeared in the Atlantic Ocean, but they are more frequent in the Pacific Ocean. Japan has suffered often from them, and scientists now call them by their Japanese name *tsunami,* which means "large waves in harbors." It's a good idea to use this word *tsunami,* because tidal waves have nothing at all to do with tides.

WHAT IS A TIDAL WAVE?

AN ORDINARY ocean wave rolls toward shore, rising and falling, until it finally spills over onto the beach. The next wave is only a few seconds behind it. Wind somewhere on the water is the main cause of these ordinary waves, although there may be only a slight breeze on the shore where they come tumbling in.

A tidal wave is different. It sweeps toward shore like a great wall of water. After it strikes, there may not be another for several minutes. Each one has tremendous force and can destroy almost anything it strikes. Many of them are thirty or forty feet high, and once a wave that hit the coast of Siberia towered up over 200 feet.

Stormy weather has nothing to do with these giant waves. They are as likely to come on a calm day as on a windy day. The force that starts them is some kind of powerful jolt underneath the water. Earthquakes often shake the rock in the bottom of the ocean. A large chunk of ocean floor may suddenly rise or drop. When the floor jumps up or down, the water above it shifts, too. The quake may start a landslide down the slope of a vast undersea canyon, and this gives water a big shove. Or a volcano may blow a hole in the ocean floor. Any of these shocks will set an enormous body of water into motion. Waves begin to travel through the sea at high speed. At four or five hundred miles an hour, they can race for thousands of miles across an entire ocean!

Ordinary waves move through the surface water. A tidal wave may reach all the way from the bottom of the sea to the top. If you are out in a ship in the middle of the ocean when a tidal wave goes by, you may not notice it all. It looks less than a foot high, and it will be gone before you can pay any attention to it. But when it comes to shallow water near shore, the wave piles up and up and then topples over with terrible force.

In the old days, no one knew when to expect tidal waves. About forty have struck Hawaii in the last 140 years. Now there are earthquake detectors all over the world. As soon as scientists know about a quake that may cause big waves, they send out warnings. People who live near the shore in the path of the wave have a chance to hurry away to higher ground.

HOW BIG IS A MOUNTAIN TOP?

THE TOPS OF some mountains are so small that there is hardly enough space to stand on. Other mountains have tops large enough to hold a base-ball field. Some tops are even larger.

A very large, flat high place is called a plateau. Smaller flat-topped rises in the land are called buttes or mesas. The people who live nearby usually decide which word to use. There is no exact rule that tells how wide a mountain top has to be before you should call it a plateau, or how small a plateau has to be before you should call it a butte or a mesa.

MOUNTAINS WERE MADE by great upward pushes that came from inside the earth. Mountains are still being made. But the pushes are usually very slow and gradual. They may go on for thousands and millions of years. So no one can feel a mountain rising up underneath his feet.

What can there be inside the earth that pushes upward with such force? There is hot, liquid rock. In some places underneath the earth's hard outside crust this liquid melts its way upward. But before it reaches the top, it spreads out sideways between two layers of solid rock. This is as if you squirted a soft sandwich filling between two slices of bread. A thick filling makes the top of the rock sandwich bulge up higher and higher.

At first this bulge may not look at all like a mountain. It may be very smooth and wide and long — more like the prairie. But in time the mountains do appear. After a long while, rain and rivers wear away channels in the raised-up rock. There are ridges between the channels of the streams and rivers, and the highest points on these ridges are mountain peaks.

Sometimes the liquid rock melts its way up and up, along a crack or a weak place, until it squirts out on top of the earth. There it builds up into a cone-shaped peak which we call a volcano.

Another kind of mountain-building happens because the rocks in the bottom of the ocean are particularly heavy. The rock on land is much lighter. The pull of gravity on the heavy rock makes the ocean bottom sink. Like a see-saw, mountains rise up on land.

Pressures from inside have also made the surface of the earth wrinkle up in fold after fold. It is not easy to believe that rock can bend and fold, but that is just what happens. Some whole mountain ranges are made of folded rock.

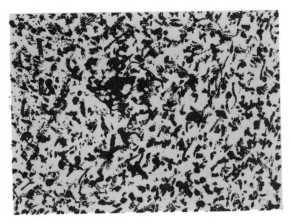
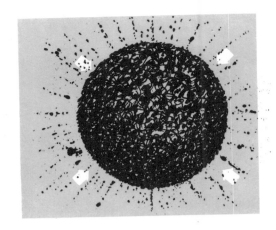

WHAT MAKES THE WORLD ROUND?

WHEN YOU LOOK out of the window, you see houses, streets, trees and fields. You may see a hill or a mountain. There are lots of sights outside your window, but nothing that makes the world look the least bit round. The world doesn't even look round when you are on the ocean, where nothing can get in the way of your view. But under the ocean, and under all the houses and streets and mountains, the world is a roundish ball. The only reason we can't see its ball-shape is that we are too close to it.

If you were up very high in the air in a plane or balloon or a space capsule, you could see the roundness that is hidden from you down on earth. Photographs taken from high up show that the earth is just as round as the moon, which we can see very easily because it's very far away.

The earth got its rounded shape ages ago when it was being formed. All the material in it came together in a great lump and this material has been held together ever since by a force called gravity. Gravity pulls everything toward the center of the lump. When a great many bits of material are all being pulled at the same time toward the same spot, they crowd together in the shape of a ball. That is what happened when the earth was being formed.

The outside of the great ball hardened into a crust of rock that is a little like the skin of an orange. The bumps and dimples on the orange skin are like the mountains and valleys on the earth. But no orange is a perfect sphere, and neither is the earth. It spins around like a top, and the spinning causes a force that pulls *against* gravity. This makes the earth swell out a little around the middle.

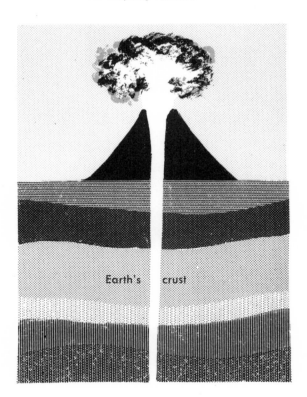

An erupting volcano

Earth's crust

IN THE UNITED STATES the chances are very, very small that you will ever see an active volcano near your home, unless you live in Hawaii or Alaska. Both these states have volcanoes that shoot out hot melted rock now and then. There is only one other state where a volcano has erupted since Columbus discovered America. Lassen Peak, in California, shot off several times between 1914 and 1917.

Most of the volcanoes in the world are found in two areas. One of these is around the shores of the Pacific Ocean. The other is a band that circles the world north of the equator. Along these two lines the hard outside crust of the earth seems to be weak. Hot liquid rock from inside comes to the surface more easily than in other places. But there have been volcanoes far from these active spots — in New Mexico and Arizona, for example. There are also volcanoes today in Iceland and on the bottom of some of the oceans.

Perhaps you've read a story about an island in the Indian Ocean called Krakatoa where a volcano exploded. The volcano was real. In the year 1883 it blew up most of the island. People three thousand miles away heard the sound of the explosion which was probably the biggest in the history of the world. Dust and ash from the volcano traveled all the way around the earth.

142

HOW DEEP IS
THE DEEPEST OCEAN?

IF WE COULD drain all the water out of the ocean, we would see marvelous sights — high mountains, vast plains and great deep gorges. These gorges have very steep sides, like the Grand Canyon in Arizona, but some of them go down much farther into the earth. One ocean canyon, called the Challenger Deep, is near the island of Guam in the Pacific Ocean. Its bottom is 35,800 feet below the surface of the water. That's nearly seven miles, and it is the deepest spot anybody has found anywhere in any ocean.

A sonar machine tells how deep the oceans are. Sonar sends sounds down through water, then measures how long they take to bounce back up again. Scientists know how fast sound travels in water, so they can figure out how far it is to the bottom. By taking many measurements with sonar, it is possible to tell exactly where underwater mountains and canyons lie and how big they are.

Two scientists in a special kind of submarine called a bathyscaph have gone to the bottom of the Challenger Deep, the lowest known spot in the world.

143

Fishermen stretch nets like this across the Bay of Fundy. At high tide the sea covers the nets. At low tide the men drive out in wagons and gather the fish that have been caught.

WHAT MAKES TIDES?

IT IS AN exciting thing to stand on a sandy ocean beach and watch the tide come in. For a while you may not realize that water is creeping up onto the land. Then you notice a dark, damp patch where there was only dry sand a minute ago. A wave reaches your toes. The next one pours over your feet. The whole ocean seems to be rising higher and higher.

A tremendous force is at work, making so much water move. That force is gravity.

The earth, the moon and the sun all have gravity. Each one pulls on the others. As the moon tugs at the earth, it tugs at everything on the earth's surface — including water, of course.

Why doesn't it pull the water right off into space? The reason is that the earth's gravity is also at work. The earth pulls more strongly than the moon does. And so the ocean only bulges toward the moon, instead of flying off the earth entirely.

The sun also tugs at the oceans, but since it is farther away than the moon, its pull is not so strong. It is mainly the moon that starts the water moving. But once it has started, something else happens. An ocean is something like a bowl of water. If you have ever tried to carry a bowl of water, you know that the water may slosh back and forth, going up and down on the sides of the bowl as you walk. It will keep on doing this for a while after you set the bowl down on a table. Your body gives movement to the water, and then that movement goes on by itself for a while. The moon gives movement to the ocean, and it then goes on rocking back and forth slowly, making tides.

On the island of Tahiti, the tide only rises once a day. In other places it rises twice a day, but only a foot or so. And in the Bay of Fundy, there are two high tides each day, and each one may have a rise of 50 feet.

You have to be a special scientist called an oceanographer before you can figure out all the different things that go into making tides behave the way they do.

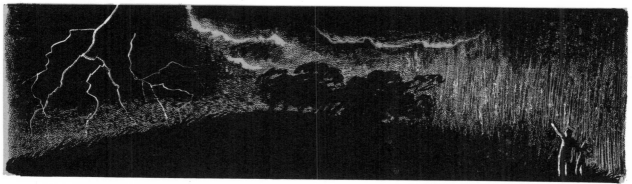

IS HEAT LIGHTNING THE SAME AS OTHER KINDS OF LIGHTNING?

THE LIGHTNING that we see during a rainstorm is called *forked* lightning. Thunder comes along after each lightning stroke.

When people talk about *heat* lightning or *sheet* lightning, they mean the flashes that appear without any thunder in hot weather, like sheets of light in the distant sky. This kind is really the same as forked lightning. We just don't hear its thunder because we are too far away. We don't actually see the lightning, either. We see its light reflected from clouds. The lightning itself struck somewhere out of sight.

WHAT IS SEA LEVEL?

WE SAY THAT the top of the highest mountain is 29,028 feet above sea level, or that Death Valley in California is 282 feet below sea level. We say that the surface of the ocean — any ocean — is at sea level. But exactly where is the surface of the sea? It is always moving. Even if there are no waves, not even any ripples, the top of the water is always moving either up or down. The tides keep it from staying at the same height.

Scientists measure this up-and-down motion with special instruments called tide gauges. They keep records of the highest high tide and the lowest high tide, and then they figure out what the average is. They do the same for the low tides. The point halfway between average high tide and average low tide is called sea level.

WHY ARE THERE SO MANY DIAMOND MINES IN AFRICA?

A GREAT MANY diamonds have been found in Africa, but they come from other places, too. India and Brazil had diamond mines before Africa did. There are mines today in the Soviet Union and in the United States at Murfeesboro, Arkansas. Experts feel sure there are many diamonds waiting to be discovered somewhere in Canada, too.

Scientists can now make small artificial diamonds. Before long, it may be cheaper to manufacture them than to mine them.

The natural diamonds were made inside volcanoes where there was great heat. So the best mines are in the rock that formed when these volcanoes cooled down. One part of Africa has a number of them. In some places the old volcano rock was worn away by rivers or glaciers. When this happened, diamonds were carried far from the places where they were made. That's why they sometimes are found in banks of sand or mud or gravel.

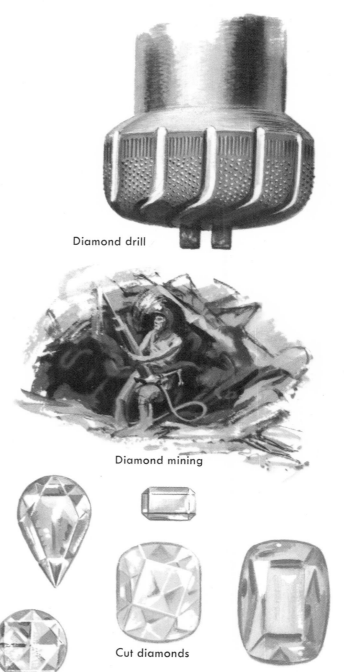

Diamond drill

Diamond mining

Cut diamonds

Diamonds are expensive jewels, but more of them are sold to factories than to jewelry stores. The reason is that diamonds are the hardest things in the world. Men use them to cut steel and other very tough metals, and to make the oil-well drills that bore holes down through solid rock.

THERE IS MORE water than land on the surface of the earth. There is more rock than water underneath the surface. If we take the earth and the planets and the sun and all the stars and all the space between them, we have to say that there is more of a gas called hydrogen than anything else. That's not all. Some scientists believe that everything in the universe came from hydrogen. Rocks that are hard and water that is wet both came from a gas that you can't feel or see! Of course, it took billions of years for the gas to change into something else that finally changed into rocks and water — and you.

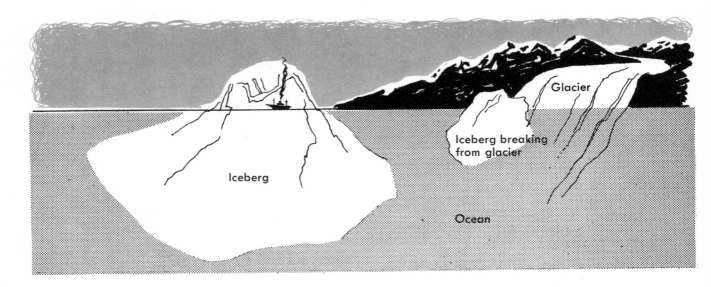

WHAT IS AN ICEBERG?

IN SOME PARTS of the world the weather is very cold all year round. Summers are so cold that a good deal of the winter snow never melts. Instead, it piles up higher and higher, year after year. Heavy top layers press down on layers underneath. Their great weight squashes the feathery snowflakes together and turns them to ice.

Each new snowfall adds more pressure and makes more ice. This ice is solid, of course, but not as stiff and unbending as you might think. It bulges out, and it can actually flow downhill, the way water flows in a river. It becomes what is called a glacier.

In many places glaciers flow right down to the sea. At the ocean's edge, big chunks of glacier break off. These chunks are often as big as mountains, and they are called icebergs. The name means ice mountains.

An iceberg floating in the sea doesn't look nearly as big as it really is. Only a small part of it shows above the surface. The rest is under water, out of sight.

WHAT MAKES SOME ROCKS DIFFERENT FROM OTHERS?

ROCKS, PEOPLE, PLANTS, air—everything in the world is made of substances called elements. There are about a hundred elements, and they can join together in countless combinations. Some elements and combinations of elements are called minerals. A nail is made of minerals and so is a glass bottle and a brick. So are TV aerials, bathtubs, concrete sidewalks, and a million other things.

Hundreds of different minerals were formed long ago when the earth was first starting. They collected in tiny bits or huge lumps. They got mixed together in thousands of different ways, and finally they hardened into what we call rocks.

The element called oxygen is a gas. When it joined with an element called silicon, the two together formed a mineral called quartz. Then quartz mixed with other minerals and made a rock called granite. But frost and rain and rivers wore granite down, and the quartz in it became grains of sand. This sand collected in lakes or along rivers or at the edge of the sea. After a long time it got cemented together and made another kind of rock — sandstone. That's the story of some of the different rocks you see around you. Other combinations and changes made the other rocks.

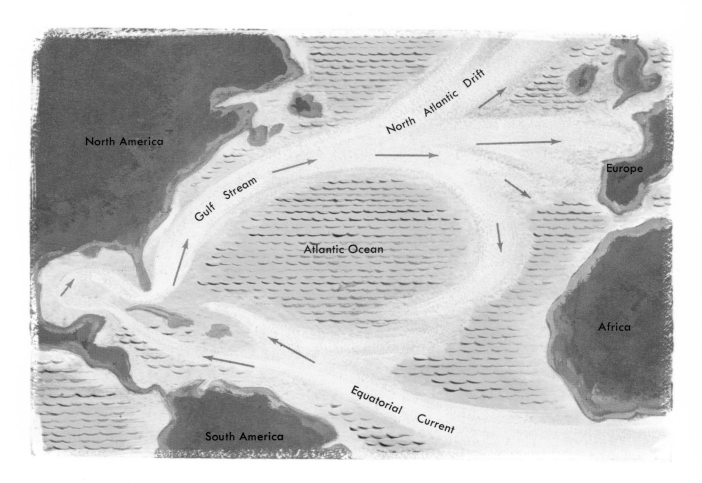

WHAT MAKES THE GULF STREAM?

THE GULF STREAM is something like a warm river that flows between walls of cold water in the Atlantic Ocean. Of course, the water in the Gulf Stream is salty, not fresh. It moves along as fast as you usually walk — which is about three miles an hour. In some places it is a hundred miles wide and a mile deep. That is a lot of water — and a lot of warmth. Summer and winter, this giant river in the sea carries heat toward the cold northern parts of the world.

When sailors first discovered the Gulf Stream, they asked, "What makes it move?" Scientists are still searching for the whole answer, but they have found out this much:

The wind and the water along the equator are moving toward the west. Some of this westward-moving water reaches the Caribbean Sea and the Gulf of Mexico, where it piles up. At one place the water is eighteen inches higher than in the open ocean where it came from.

150

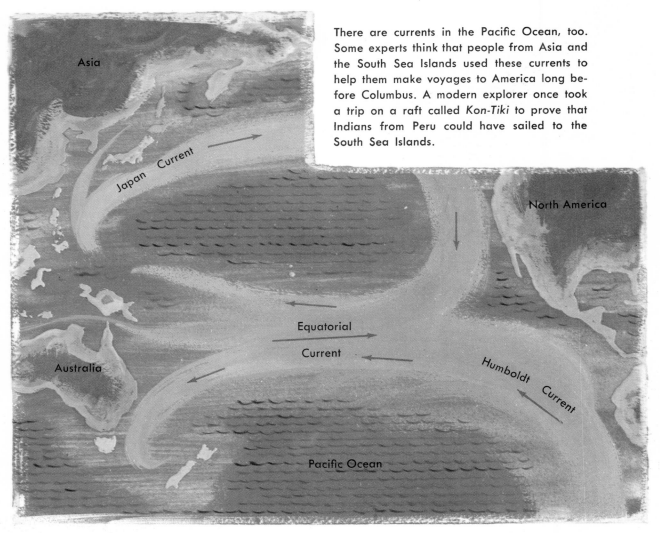

There are currents in the Pacific Ocean, too. Some experts think that people from Asia and the South Sea Islands used these currents to help them make voyages to America long before Columbus. A modern explorer once took a trip on a raft called *Kon-Tiki* to prove that Indians from Peru could have sailed to the South Sea Islands.

Of course, the water that keeps piling up in the Gulf of Mexico has to keep spilling out. It pours through the space between Cuba and Florida, and that is the beginning of the Gulf Stream. From there, winds help to move it along toward the north.

While this warm water is heading northward, cold water from the Arctic is heading southward. Because cold water is heavy, most of it flows deep down in the Atlantic Ocean, *under* the Gulf Stream. But some of it flows alongside the Gulf Stream, and in spots it even flows in the *middle* of the Gulf Stream!

The warm Gulf Stream keeps flowing northward, and some of it goes all the way past Norway. More of it turns and goes down the eastern side of the ocean, and then comes back across near the equator. The water moves round and round like a gigantic slow-motion whirlpool.

WHY DOES FROST ON WINDOWS LOOK LIKE FERNS?

IF THE WEATHER is very cold outdoors, you may see frost on your windowpanes. The frost is made of tiny bits of ice, and the ice came from moisture floating about in the air. When moisture meets the cold glass, it forms ice crystals. Sometimes the crystals make a plain white coat upon the window. But they may appear in beautiful leafy shapes, as if a garden of ice ferns had sprouted during the night.

Scientists have made ice crystals inside bottles in a laboratory, and they have found that the shapes seem to depend on the temperature. When it goes down to a little below freezing, the crystals are flat, six-sided plates. If it is colder, the crystals are shaped like needles, then like hollow six-sided tubes. When it gets very, very cold, the branched, leafy shapes appear. Still, nobody knows for sure just why these things happen. Perhaps the frost ferns start to grow along fine scratches in the glass. Or the moisture from the air may collect in special ways around specks of dust on the window, or on a little film of soap left from window washing.

HOW DO WE FIND OUT?

Ever since the first cave man had hiccups, people have wondered about themselves and the world they live in. Why are things the way they are, instead of some other way? What makes this happen or that happen? And how can we find answers to all our questions?

Gradually people have discovered that there are many ways to find answers. Here are some that you can use yourself.

1. *Ask questions.* Ask your mother. Ask your father. Ask your teacher. Ask the librarian. Go to a museum and ask. Look in books, for that is another way of asking. And keep asking. That is what scientists do.

A scientist does something else. He keeps on asking questions even after an answer has turned up. He doesn't believe the first answer he hears. He wants proof. This sometimes makes him a very annoying person to have around. You also may find that if you ask a great many questions, some people will think you are a nuisance. What can you do about that? The best thing is to ask questions only when you really care about answers.

2. *Watch carefully.* A scientist looks at things with his own eyes. He is not satisfied to learn what others say they have seen. He often looks through a magnifying glass or a microscope or a telescope, so that he can see as much as can possibly be seen. And as he looks, he doesn't just guess at the size and shape and speed of things. He measures, weighs, counts.

3. *Try out explanations.* After you have asked a question and done your watching, you may have an answer that seems to make sense. But is it really the right answer? Sometimes you can try out an idea. There are good books of scientific experiments that you can do at home. If you learn how to do these, you can go on and get many answers for youself.

INDEX

Numerals in italics refer to pictures.
Entries printed in capital letters refer to question-titles.

What Is an Iceberg

What Makes a Baseball Curve?

Are Race Horses Different From Other Horses?